THE LAST CAUCUS
IN IOWA

The Last Caucus in Iowa

Jim O'Loughlin

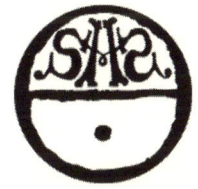

Ice Cube Press, LLC (Est. 1991)
North Liberty, Iowa, USA

The Last Caucus in Iowa: 20+ candidates and the start of the 2020 election

Copyright ©2020 Jim O'Loughlin

First Edition

ISBN 9781948509206

Library of Congress Control Number: 2020944867

Ice Cube Press, LLC (Est. 1991)
1180 Hauer Drive
North Liberty, Iowa 52317 USA
www.icecubepress.com | steve@icecubepress.com

All rights reserved.

No portion of this book may be reproduced in any way without permission, except for brief quotations for review, or educational work, in which case the publisher shall be provided copies. The views expressed in *The Last Caucus in Iowa* are solely those of the author, not the Ice Cube Press, LLC.

The paper used in this publication meets the minimum requirements of the American National Standard for Information Sciences—Permanence of Paper for Printed Library Materials, ANSI Z39.48-1992.

Manufactured in USA

Foreword, 7

Introduction, 9

Part I: The Candidates, 13

    Chapter 1: Elizabeth Warren, 14

    Chapter 2: Julián Castro, 20

    Chapter 3: Kirstin Gillibrand, 25

    Chapter 4: Cory Booker, 30

    Chapter 5: Eric Swalwell, 36

    Chapter 6: Steve Bullock, 41

    Chapter 7: Beto O'Rourke, 46

    Chapter 8: Pete Buttigieg, 51

    Chapter 9: Amy Klobuchar, 56

    Chapter 10: Bernie Sanders, 61

    Chapter 11: Bill de Blasio, 66

    Chapter 12: John Hickenlooper, 71

    Chapter 13: Kamala Harris, 77

    Chapter 14: Tulsi Gabbard, 82

    Chapter 15: Joe Sestak, 87

    Chapter 16: Michael Bennet, 92

    Chapter 17: Joe Biden, 98

    Chapter 18, 19 & 20: Marianne Williamson, Tom Steyer, John Delaney, 103

    Chapter 21: Andrew Yang, 112

Part II: The Caucus, 119

    Chapter 22: Memories of Caucuses Past I [Introduction and 2000], 120

    Chapter 23: Memories of Caucuses Past II [2004], 122

    Chapter 24: Memories of Caucuses Past III [2008], 126

    Chapter 25: Memories of Caucuses Past IV [2016], 133

    Chapter 26: Caucus Night 2020, 137

Conclusion: The Last Caucus in Iowa, 162

Foreword

The Last Caucus in Iowa was not an intentional project. It began when I remembered how much out-of-state friends appreciated social media posts I had made during the night of the Iowa Caucus in 2016. From the outside looking in (and even when you're involved), the caucus seems a puzzling occasion, and my friends appreciated an inside view. In January 2019, Elizabeth Warren became the first major candidate to announce that she was running for the Democratic nomination, and my family and I went to see her on her initial swing through Iowa. I made similar social media posts, and people were still interested.

    I realized that by live posting an event, I had done a fair portion of the work that would be involved if I wanted to create a blog. A blog was more of a commitment than just a few posts here and there. That would involve seeing many candidates, but since I expected that many events would happen close to home, I felt it was doable. Though I ended up driving around the state more than I anticipated, the "20+ Candidates" blog lived up to its name as I was able to see 21 people running for President over the course of the caucus season, including almost all of the candidates with a national profile. In a few cases, people dropped out before I could get to their events (Jay Inslee, we hardly knew ye). But that experience serves as the core of this book, building up to the night of the caucus itself and beyond.

What was originally intended to be a concluding chapter has been expanded into a second section of the book that asks some questions about the caucus process and what its future might be, both because of the difficulties in determining the results of this cycle's caucus and in light of the COVID-19 outbreak, which is happening as I am writing these lines. As for this book's title… well, we'll see. Maybe this will be the final Presidential caucus in Iowa or at least the final first-in-the-nation caucus. Calls for the end to Iowa's prominent role have only grown in light of the tabulation problems on caucus night. But perhaps those concerns will recede or be resolved over time. It also is possible that "last" may come to mean just "the most recent," which would still make the title accurate. Either way, that's my title and I'm sticking with it.

My thanks to members of my family, my wife (Julie) and our children (Nic, Devin and Ian) who accompanied me on many of the candidate visits and allowed me to turn them into characters in this evolving narrative. They were good sports throughout the whole process, and our dinner table conversations benefitted from all that we saw together.

Introduction

A note of explanation: the first section of this book expands and modifies material that originally appeared in the 20+ Candidates blog. When I attended a candidate event, I tried to take notes, shoot images and video, and post some of my observations to social media. It usually took me about a week to put together the accompanying blog post for each event. This is a work of creative nonfiction, which means that while I've detailed events and experiences that actually took place, I don't let that get in the way of a good joke.

In preparing these chapters for the book, I've resisted the temptation to use hindsight to make my initial impressions even more perceptive. But it is a temptation. It would have been funny if I could have foregrounded the Buttigieg/Klobuchar feud or shown the head of the Iowa Democratic Party fumbling with an app on his phone. However, those things didn't happen. The American Eagle flying over the Joe Biden event? Yeah, that really did happen.

I am not a journalist, and this is not a work of journalism. Nothing against such work, it's just not what this book is. I did not have press credentials for any event I attended, and what I experienced was what anyone else who took the time to see as many Presidential candidates as possible could have seen. Though I aimed to detail what was interesting or noteworthy in what candidates had to say, my focus was just as much on the process. The one thing everyone knows about Iowa is that since it has the first-in-the-nation caucus, Iowa (fairly or not) receives an outsized share of attention. But it's not as if there is an infrastructure in place for dozens of candidates to visit the state. Each campaign has to reinvent the wheel, as venues and potential caucus goers orient themselves to this phenomenon that happens once every four years. The varied workings of this process proved to be at least as interesting as what the candidates had to say.

It's important to know something about Iowa's role with the first-in-the-nation caucus: it doesn't really make sense. A recent Raygun t-shirt captures this dynamic with the slogan, "Iowa! For some reason, you have to come here to be President!" If one was creating an electoral process from scratch, this isn't how you would do it. The whole thing always seems a little ramshackle and thrown together, like finding out last minute that you've agreed to host a party at your house. "What? Do we have enough clean plates? Is there any wine in the refrigerator?"

Of course, that's also what makes it interesting. Every four years, in the state that I've called home for almost 20 years, I have to reorient my sense of what it means to be here. For example, I live in Cedar Falls, a small city/college town in the northeast part of the state. It's a great place to live, and I can give you lots of reasons to come visit, but if you're not from here, you're likely to say something like "Is that the same thing as Cedar Rapids?" Uh…no. But every four years, presidential candidates traverse the state, and any place with a sizable population and available space for rallies becomes an attraction.

Basically, I don't expect anyone from outside Iowa to know where I live, but I'm also not surprised when a nationally-recognized politician gladhands it through the crowd at a bar within walking distance of my house.

On the one hand, this whole process was unusual, and it only got weirder the closer I was to it. However, on the other hand, this election couldn't be more serious. There's a reason more than 20 candidates tossed a hat in the ring. How could you be a politician with any experience and a national reputation and not consider running? If you are reading this book, and even if you have nothing to do with politics, you've probably watched Donald Trump and thought "WTF? I could do better than that!"

In what follows, I often view political events a bit skeptically, looking for humor to alleviate the experience of standing in lines or being crowded into rooms not designed for the events they are hosting. But this book is not snarky about candidates and their desire to run for higher office. There's plenty of snark out there, and you can find that if you need it. Sure, I was drawn to some candidates more than others, and I get that politicians can be driven by vanity and calculation, but I also knew going in that one of these people was going to be all that separates us from a second Donald Trump term. The stakes are high and the results are unpredictable. I was not going to prejudge.

So, bring it on. Big rallies, small house parties, candidate selfies, firm handshaking, potlucks and long speeches. I'm in for all of it.

Part One

The Candidates

Chapter 1

Elizabeth Warren
[5 January 2019]

Massachusetts Senator Elizabeth Warren was the first top-tier candidate to announce that she was running for President, and it was surprising that her launch came right at the start of 2019. Beginning a campaign more than a year before the Iowa Caucus seemed earlier than necessary to me, but it did ensure that Warren would have the corner on media coverage. Her launch schedule also was unexpected. She clustered her initial events in western Iowa, the most conservative part of the state where Steve King is the U. S. representative. Des Moines was the closest she was going to get to those of us in the bluer, eastern part of the state.

It was winter break, and Julie and I had been wanting to get out of town anyway, so we decided to make an overnight trip of it for the whole family. We spent the day milling about Des Moines's East Village and ate at Zombie Burger. It was a Sunday afternoon so there wasn't a whole lot going on, but it was an unseasonably nice day, so we didn't mind walking around the city, and all three of the kids, Nic, Devin and Ian, were on board for the event.

When Nic wanted to get there an hour before the event was scheduled to begin to ensure a good spot, I didn't object. Devin had last campaign's Mt. Nasty t-shirt for the occasion (it had Elizabeth Warren as one of the faces on a female Mt. Rushmore), and Ian was up for the wait as well. The event was at a location called Curate, and when we got there I saw what looked like a converted warehouse, which could now be rented for hipster weddings. There was already a line in front of the event center/warehouse when we took our places at the end.

It was late afternoon, which I realized suddenly when I saw a guy in front of me with a cup of coffee. I had not had any coffee. About five minutes later, Devin said she was thirsty. I saw my chance. I looked online for the nearest coffee shop and told Devin she could go get something to drink if she brought me back a coffee. Ian was getting squirmy, so he went with her. After they left, I texted them to use a bathroom while they had the chance.

The line to get in continued to grow, turning a corner. I think a line has to go around two corners before it can be said to be "wrapping around the block," and it never made it quite that far, but it was still a good turnout. I noticed that the vibe in the line was not at all like rallies or protests early in the Trump presidency. People weren't angry, and they weren't cynical. While it is common for Iowans to complain about the length of the election season, particularly when broadcast TV becomes dominated by campaign ads, there was none of that. People were just anxious to get started already. Call it the Trump Effect.

Whenever the door to the event center opened, we would look up with anticipation, hoping we were about to be allowed inside. Alas, time and again, we would see the door slam shut after a staffer scurried in. But eventually the door truly did open to the public, the line did begin moving, and we finally got inside. It was a multi-purpose space with a stage against the far wall and a concrete floor that I could see was not going to be enjoyable to stand on. But we didn't take time to look around, because the main point of getting there early was to get a good spot in front of the stage. We pushed our way as far forward as we could and waited while the crowd filled in behind us.

And we waited. We talked, we played on our phones, we took turns squatting on the floor when our backs got sore. No political event in the history of political events has ever started on time, and this one was no exception. Ian announced that he had, in fact, not gone to the bathroom at the coffee shop. As I looked at the crowd between us and the bathroom, I grew concerned that this might not end well. At one point, Elizabeth Warren tried to take a peek out at the crowd from behind the stage curtain. That never works. People saw her and started cheering, but to no avail. We continued to wait. Eventually, we got loopy. Ian and Devin began playing around with a faceswapping app. Here's a picture of me with Nic's beard. Other pictures were weirder than that.

When the song "9 to 5" began playing loudly from the speakers, I thought maybe it was a sign that things were ready to begin, but that was a false hope. Then, just when it seemed like the event would never start, it began. Elizabeth Warren took the stage to a big cheer from the crowd, and immediately she told us that she had a cold and her voice was shot. This is actually pretty common among presidential candidates, so no one expected it to make a difference.

It didn't. Warren began with a personal story, talking about growing up in Oklahoma in a working class family that had had some close-to-the-edge times. She made powerful connections between her career and the big policy decisions (like a meaningful minimum wage and support for education) that made it possible for her to have one.

"When I was a kid, a minimum wage job would support a family of three… Today, a minimum wage job in America—full time—will not keep a mama and her baby out of poverty. That is wrong and it's why I'm in this fight."

As she was speaking, I realized that Elizabeth Warren's personal story wasn't as well known, and I wondered if it was something that would play more of a role during the campaign.

What put Warren on the progressive side of this race was that she was not looking just to get back to how things were during the Obama years. She was forthright about aiming to make changes that go far beyond just undoing the damage of the current administration.

"We need change, but not just one statute here or one law over there. That's not going to get the job done. We need big, structural change. We've got to go big."

She laid out some of her key proposals for attacking corruption and unfair policies. Her targets included the revolving door between politics and lobbying, Citizens United, and health care costs. There were a lot of targets.

Warren had plenty to say about policy and, as expected, she could give chapter and verse of legislation as needed. But she also had an eye for what issues were likely to be most persuasive, and the crowd was glad to respond to her applause lines like this one:

"My daddy ended up as a janitor, and I got a chance to become a public school teacher, a college professor, and a United States senator because America invested in opportunity for me. I am determined that we will be a country that invests in opportunity for every one of our children."

She finished the stump speech part of the event to a big round of applause. It was noteworthy that Trump's name never came up in her remarks. Warren seemed to be going by the theory that when you're talking about Trump you're losing. And, in fact, the media coverage of this event zeroed in on the one audience question that referenced Trump.

The Q&A was done via lottery. When we came in, we all got a ticket, and numbers were called out for the lucky winners to step up to one of the audience microphones. Most of the audience questions were on specific policy issues, such as separation of church and state, college student debt, and housing costs. There are no end of challenges to take on at this moment in time. The issue was which ones come first.

That would have been my question for her: "where do you begin?" but though I had a ticket for a lottery to ask a question, my number wasn't called.

However, when the event ended after about an hour, we were close to the stage, and we were able to push to the front for pictures.

Picture taking was a serious operation for the Warren campaign with an assembly line of staffers to control the crowd, grab our jackets, and take a picture. The Senator had pledged not to leave until everyone who wanted a candidate selfie got one. She was all in with seemingly inexhaustible enthusiasm as we wormed our way to the stage with her and all got our shots taken. Warren complimented Devin on her t-shirt, which may have made the whole trip worthwhile for her (though as an added bonus, when a *Time* magazine article on Warren's initial Iowa swing came out the next week, there was a picture with our four identifiable faces among the hundreds in the crowd).

Afterward, we made our way into the now-cooler night. It had been almost three years since the last Presidential election. Finally, I felt like the next campaign had begun.

Chapter 2

Julián Castro
[7 January 2019]

If you're not from Iowa, here's something you might not expect: it's not unusual for a non-rock star candidate to have events in coffee shops or book stores or at the house of a supporter. So, I was not surprised to see that Julián Castro, former Obama administration HUD secretary and San Antonio mayor, was having a pre-announcement event at someone's house near Cedar Rapids.

There is a charm in these smaller meet-and-greets that make running for President seem a little bit more like trying to get elected to City Council. If nothing else, it was sure to be a different experience from the big Elizabeth Warren launch we had just gone to. Nic and I drove down, hoping the GPS would be able to get us to a house on Lois Lane, and I had a ready supply of Superman jokes if necessary.

The GPS came through for us, as we realized when we saw cars lined up on both sides of a wooded exurban street. When we got to the house where the event was being held, we realized we were just supposed to open the door and walk in. We did. I was expecting to be besieged by a staffer doing everything legally possible to obtain my email address, but this was way more casual. A crowd of about 30 people were just milling around the first floor. There was a nice spread of snacks. It felt like going to a neighborhood holiday party except there were a half-dozen TV cameras pointing at a spot in front of the living room bookcase where, until the candidate arrived, a lot of lenses were focused on books about Impressionism and the American Civil War.

Nic and I looked around for good sight lines. Fortunately, the house had an open concept layout, and we were able to get a decent view over the cameras from the kitchen. Now, Iowa may not be the largest state, but if you're an hour from home and standing in a stranger's kitchen, you still are unlikely to know anyone. Nic and I hung together, exchanging some small talk about all the TV cameras with people next to us. We were far enough out of the city that I couldn't get a phone signal. I wrote a bunch of social media posts that began piling up in a queue.

I was ready for another long wait before the candidate actually spoke, but this event ran pretty close to schedule. Julián Castro swept in through the front door, shook some hands on his way through the dining room, and found his mark in front of the bookcase. He was dressed in standard "candidate casual" with an open collar shirt and slacks that was still more formal than the rest of us (Iowa's "come as you are" fashion will have to be the subject of a future chapter).

Castro was an engaging guy, and he combined details of his family's personal story with policy issues. We found out that he was born 10 minutes before his twin brother, U. S. Rep. Joaquin Castro. He seemed much more interested in talking about being a city mayor than about his work as HUD secretary. Like Elizabeth Warren, he made a point of hammering home issues related to the minimum wage.

"We haven't had a minimum wage increase in almost 10 years. We need to raise the minimum wage in our country so that everybody can get ahead," Castro said to applause, "and not only people at the top."

Unlike Warren, he was willing to spend time specifically targeting the Trump administration. "What I see in our country today is that for the first time in a long time we're going backward not forward. We have leadership in Washington D.C., in the White House, that is so determined to divide Americans instead of unite them, that is so determined to pick and choose who gets opportunity and who doesn't, based on your faith or something else, that's so determined to go backward."

It was a crowd of political junkies, so we would have been happy to listen for quite a while, but Castro kept it short and took a bunch of questions. I was able to ask the last one, and I urged him to draw on his experience as HUD secretary to let us know "what you would want us to know about how HUD has functioned under Ben Carson and what needs to happen there in the future."

My question provoked some laughs from the crowd as there had recently been a minor scandal in the news about HUD purchasing a table and chairs for more than $30,000, and this was happening in the midst of a temporary government shutdown. Castro picked up on that vibe, and since he was good enough to give a detailed answer to my question, I'm reproducing his response here in full.

"You want to know about the dining set? I read an article yesterday that said that 95% of the HUD employees, basically the functions of HUD, are furloughed right now, and that soon if the shutdown doesn't end, that landlords that do the Section 8 program, that rent an affordable place to families, that they're not going to get their checks, and at that point they may just withdraw and start evicting tenants.

So, now, this is just one example, but to answer your question, what I've seen is a lack of commitment to serving the people that that department is supposed to serve. They've proposed a six-million dollar budget cut to the department, even though we have a rental affordability crisis in this country, even though you can see more people sleeping on the streets. During the Obama administration, between 2010 and 2016, there was a 47% reduction in veteran homelessness because President Obama made it a priority to work with mayors and governors across the country to try to get to effective zero on veteran homelessness. And there were 36 communities in three states that actually did get to effective zero. This last year, veteran homelessness actually went up in this country. And so we're going in the wrong direction.

At a time when we need to be investing in housing that is affordable for people who are poor and for the middle class, they want to cut the budget. At a time when you need folks that are committed to the mission of the organization, I think you have a lot of people there like the person that is running the New York office who used to be the party planner for the Trumps. She was the event planner for the family, and then they made her the top HUD official for the most significant office outside of headquarters, which is the New York/New Jersey regional office. New York is the most active HUD-related big city in the United States. There is a lack of concern for the people that they're trying to serve. It's just going in the wrong direction, and I completely disagree with it."

Then Castro said something that I thought was really important and that I had not heard discussed elsewhere regarding the challenges that would face the next President, who will need to pick up the pieces of the disruption of the Trump administration.

"You know, the next President is going to have to spend at least the first two years of the next administration cleaning up the mess that this administration has made, restocking those federal agencies with people who are experts and know what they are doing, going to Congress and getting the resources that we need to address these critical issues, whether it's at HUD or the Department of Transportation or Education or wherever it is, and I think also recommitting to the mission. When Ronald Reagan walked through the door in 1981, HUD had more than 16,000 employees. By the time I left, there were less than 8,000. I bet you anything that today there are less than 7,000 because it's losing people who don't think that the folks there right now believe in the mission of the organization, and I would change that."

It was a nice note to end on, and Castro was given a warm round of applause. Nic and I made our way through the kitchen and into the living room to get a picture. I appreciated that Castro understood everyone was candidate shopping, and he wasn't going to ask us to sign on to a campaign that wasn't even going to be official until next weekend. We got a couple selfies and grabbed our jackets. I felt like we should have searched around for the people who lived in this house and said thanks, the way you would if you'd been invited to a party, but they were in a different room and we had an hour to drive. We walked out into the quiet night, got in the car and drove until we got phone service again. Okay, that was not such a big deal. It only took five minutes. I debated making a joke about kryptonite jamming my phone while we were at Lois Lane, but if Julián Castro could get through the whole night without a Superman joke, so could I.

Chapter 3
Kirsten Gillibrand
[19 January 2019]

I first should note that it was not my goal to keep driving across the state to see candidates. The point was to wait for the candidates to come to where I live and then to smugly decide at the last minute whether a particular candidate was interesting enough to merit my driving across town. But this was Nic's last full day before he headed back to college in Connecticut, a blue state where one can be pretty sure no Presidential candidate is going to be doing anything other than fundraising. So, we were on the road again, headed to Des Moines the day after the first meaningful snowstorm of the year to see New York Senator Kirstin Gilliibrand during her post-exploratory-committee announcement tour of Iowa.

Fortunately, the roads were in good shape, and the two-hour drive there would be during the daytime. I pulled up the location for this event on my phone, Peace Tree Brewing Co., and I recognized it as the craft brewery across the street from the event center where we had seen Elizabeth Warren a couple weeks before. I remembered this because as I was standing in a long line outside the Warren event, I gazed longingly at the brewery across the street and thought how nice it would be to be sitting inside, having a beer. I wondered if, as at the Warren event, we would have to wait outside in a line before we would be let in to see Kirstin Gillirand. It was only 15 degrees.

I didn't have to worry. We had no problem getting in. The brewery/tasting room seemed like it would be big enough to fit a crowd of about one hundred, and it was filling up when we arrived. I got an OG Orange Sour craft beer (Nic was still 20, so only root beer for him), and we tried to figure out where the actual event was going to be. The tasting room was separated into two sections divided by a row of decorative kegs with a small sign saying that the Gillibrand event was on the other side of the kegs. The room wasn't packed yet, but all the seats were taken so we stood where we thought we'd have a good view of where the Senator would be speaking. It was hard to tell what was going on. TV cameras stationed in the room were pointed in different directions. We stood next to a table where people were playing what looked like a version of mah jongg. It wasn't clear whether they were actually here for the event.

Almost immediately, a reporter from the *Washington Post* asked if she could interview us. Sure, we were game, and we were glad to chat about politics and weather. It came out that the reporter's hometown was not far from Hartford, where Nic goes to college. In fact, she was from Longmeadow, Massachusetts. I told her I once painted a house in Longmeadow. We had a moment.

After the reporter left, we were left standing next to the not-quite-mah jongg players. I posted a picture of the table to my friends on social media, and immediately there was a flurry of discussion about rummikub, a game that may be of Dutch origin and which many of my friends played as children, setting off a round of online reminiscences. We, too, had a moment, albeit a digital one this time.

Then the waiting began. Nic and I wished we had left our jackets in the car. I finished my beer, but the room was now crowded enough that I feared not being able to get back if I tried to get another one. At one point, a staffer and someone from C-Span were literally within a foot of my face, having a conversation about where a mic should be set up. Soon, I realized that we were not standing where we would have a sightline of where the Senator would be speaking. No, we, in fact, were standing right next to where she would be speaking. Essentially, we were on the "stage."

But even as this space was being transformed for a political event, it was still a brewery tasting room with TVs scattered throughout the building. The Kentucky-Auburn basketball game was playing on one screen, and when Kentucky pulled out a close win, a random guy threw up his arms and whooped, "Who's from Kentucky here?" Crickets.

Finally, an outside door opened, suggesting that the Senator was about to arrive. Someone from C-Span tried to bump me out of the way, but I held my ground. Then, Kirstin Gillibrand did appear and made her way into the room. She wore a bright blue dress jacket, jeans, and though I don't want to make too big of a deal about what candidates wear, I feel compelled to note that Gillibrand had a great pair of boots. They were fashionable but looked Iowa winter-ready. I was able to make such careful sartorial observations because the Senator ended up standing right next me to give her speech. I made a point of trying to smile since I knew I might be on camera. Later, I saw that indeed I was right in the camera frame for the C-SPAN broadcast. I was glad I had shaved that day.

Gillibrand began by discussing her entry into politics, running in a conservative upstate New York district. One pollster had told her she wouldn't be able to win because "there are more cows than Democrats in your district." But she did win that and future races, and she argued that there was, in fact, broad support for government action on health care, prescription drug costs, and a litany of other issues.

"The problem we have right now," she continued. "that makes every bit of that impossible, is that all the levels of power are controlled by those powerful few. It is controlled by the systems of power of money and greed that dominate everything." She argued that the corrupting influence of money had made it difficult to make even very popular and needed changes that threatened the profits of small, powerful sectors. Her argument was a combative one, saying that powerful forces needed to be confronted not cajoled.

Of the candidates I'd seen so far, Gillibrand spoke the most about Trump, for example, saying that "he is spreading a darkness across America that is destroying and ripping apart the very fabric of our country." It was unclear whether this was a productive approach. There was not a single person at any of these events that needed to be persuaded to vote against Donald Trump, so it was a bit of preaching to the choir. But the choir had been waiting to sing for a while, and they were glad to applaud when Gillibrand accused Trump of "destroying the decency, the basic moral, common decency that this country has always believed in. And that is wrong."

Gillibrand's stump speech was about 15 minutes long, and then she began taking questions on issues ranging from child care to immigrant rights. Eventually, she decided to move the "stage" to the other side of the beer keg wall to address the other half of the crowd. I was happy to be off camera for a while so that I could stop smiling. On the other side of the room, she was able to answer questions about issues including working across party lines and voting rights. The crowd wasn't as large or as enthusiastic as at the Warren event I had seen across the street, but when Gillibrand gave an impassioned answer to a question about global warming, calling for a "moonshot approach" inspired John F. Kennedy's space program, she got her biggest ovation of the night.

Then, the Q&A ended and the selfie scrum began. Nic and I turned out to be poorly positioned with the decorative beer kegs between us and the Senator. Nic said we should go around the barrels on the side closest to us. This was almost a fatal mistake, really a rookie error that a seasoned politico like Nic should never have made. You always want to be between the candidate and the exit.

We joined the crowd pushing toward the candidate as she slowly made her way through the room, shaking hands and posing for pictures. Nic edged ahead of me, getting slightly closer, but I worried she would make her exit before we could intercept her. "Shout at her you were born in Buffalo!" I hoped this may be irresistible for a Senator from upstate New York. It was also true, since that's where Nic had lived for the first three months of his life.

Nic persisted, pressing his way through the crowd ahead of me. I hung back and got my phone ready for a picture. Nic was successful. He got to shake her hand, and he was also able to tell her that he was from Buffalo, all of which was captured on C-Span. That was enough to call it a day. We still had a long ride to get home, and the campaign season was really just at its start.

Chapter 4
Cory Booker [9 February 2019]

The day before, New Jersey Senator Cory Booker had visited the community college that was 15 minutes from my house, but it was when I was working, and apparently I preferred driving long distances to see candidates at craft breweries, so the next day that meant a trip to Marshalltown. The good news was that this meant my wife, Julie, and daughter, Devin, were able to come with me.

I hadn't been to Marshalltown since a tornado came through town in July of last year. It did a lot of damage, and there were still a number of crumbling buildings and half-destroyed trees. So, my sympathy goes out to Marshalltown on its long road to recovery. But, wow, these were some of the worst plowed streets I'd ever seen in my life. Though lanes were moderately cleared, the center of the roads downtown had about a two-foot pile of snow. Turning onto a side street was like breaking through an igloo.

Nevertheless, we found the craft brewery where the event was to take place and got there just in time to get three of the last remaining seats in the place. The Iowa River Craft Brewery had a homey, DIY vibe, but it was not that large a space, maybe ⅓ the size of the tasting room where I had recently seen Kirstin Gillibrand. Since things were getting pretty crowded pretty fast, I quickly shouldered my way to the bar and ordered a Belgian Ale, returning to my seat before anyone could take it. It was a good thing I hadn't wasted any time. This place was way too small for the crowd that was making its way inside.

Pretty soon, attendees were pressed in against camera operators and reporters. The camera people began negotiating to move attendees around. Someone knocked into the table next to me, jostling my beer onto the table, where it began running toward a reporter's notebook. I wiped it up quickly, but the reporter was not amused.

People kept crowding in and the room got more full. I was close enough to the guy next to me that I could have taken a sip from his beer. The woman in front of me was only a slight slip away from sitting in my lap. We began discussing fire code occupancy limits. The reporter that found my beer spill unfunny joked with the guy next to her about having him lift her to safety if there was a fire. It was possible she wasn't really joking.

Julie leaned over and noted to me that the TV people were cartoonishly attractive. This was true, although the cartoonishness may have been a result of the crazy amount of makeup TV reporters have to wear. But she thought even the camera operators were a breed apart, with distinctive George Clooney-ish square jawed kind of looks.

I dutifully noted her observation and thought nothing of it until she started chatting up a George Clooney-ish looking camera operator. Later, I gave her a hard time for flirting. She claimed she was not flirting, and that it was just her combination of adopted-Iowa-nice and native-New-York-chattiness. Our daughter, Devin, just laughed at both of us.

The camera operator turned out to have a fascinating story. He'd been all over the world, covering everything from the Olympics to episodes of *Dateline* (one of Julie's favorite guilty pleasures!). He was working with a sound engineer who was also his brother, and the two of them were going to Berlin next week. The sound engineer brother was also notably handsome, but in more of a Clark Kent way. Apparently the brothers George and Clark travelled the world having adventures together, which clearly should be turned into its own TV show someday.

Time passed. A half an hour after the event was scheduled to begin, the crowd started getting loopy. The woman right in front of me shared the results of her DNA test with a total stranger, and tried to persuade him to get tested—"You just spit into a cup and send it in," she told him. At least she apologized when she did accidentally sit in my lap.

Finally, a local state representative took the stage (really just a corner of the bar) to announce that Cory Booker was only three minutes away, and he had a handmade chess set for Booker when the Senator arrived. I had zero faith that the Senator was only three minutes away (and I was right) but eventually, the doors sprung open and in swept Cory Booker along with a gust of arctic air. Most candidates have aides that come into a room before them and clear out a path to the stage, but Cory Booker did that job himself. I think being a former football player (as he would later tell us) may have helped him break through the secondary.

He took the stage to applause, started speaking, and immediately it became clear that his voice was shot. He joked that he sounded like Sherrod Brown, a Democratic Senator from Michigan with a distinctive gravelly voice, and that was a pretty close approximation. Now, Cory Booker was no slouch at public speaking. He started off with a great story of visiting Jimmy Carter in Plains, Georgia, and followed that up with an anecdote about his parents' involvement in a housing segregation sting operation during the civil rights movement. It all culminated in a scene where an evil landlord punched a lawyer and sicced his dog on Booker's dad. Pretty decent material! Booker's approach was right out of the Obama playbook. His stump speech offered a vision of a big tent that embraced inclusive moments in American history without ignoring ugly moments from the American past.

"What does patriotism mean? It means love of country, and you cannot love your country unless you love your fellow countrymen and women. It doesn't mean we always like each other. It doesn't mean we always agree with each other. But love says that I see you, I see your dignity, I see your human worth, and I know that my destiny and your destiny are interwoven. We're in this together."

Though it seemed like Booker's voice could give out at any moment, he made it through a half hour stump speech and said he'd better get to questions from the audience when he could still speak. People had questions! He was asked about child care costs, drug prices, and racial animosity in America.

His impulse to include discordant views led him to a weird moment when he talked about trying to be understanding to those who didn't understand why people are offended by blackface (there had recently been revelations in the news about prominent politicians who had been photographed wearing blackface when they were younger).

"I've had conversations with white friends of mine this week who had the safety to come to me and ask me, 'I don't understand this blackface thing, can you explain it to me?' Imagine in this climate now, saying that publically?... Put yourself in a white person's position who might have questions?"

A number of media outlets saw this thought experiment as a bridge too far, and Booker was criticized for it afterward. As these things go, this one oddly discordant instance became the main part of the speech that received coverage, and only those who were in attendance got to see the more impressive rhetorical moments, which was too bad, because there were many.

Then, as if he had an egg timer in his pocket, at almost precisely the one hour mark, Booker concluded with a stem winder that brought the audience to its feet.

"We are Americans. This election is going to be about a lot of things. It's going to be about health care: we will do better. It's going to be about public education: we will create cathedrals of learning. It's going to be about our veterans. It's going to be about jobs with dignity. It's going to be about a lot of things, but underlying all of that, ladies and gentlemen, is this idea of 'what will the American spirit be? What will the American character be?' And I believe the spirit of our country—as imperfect, as much as we've stumbled and tripped sometimes along the pathway—the spirit, the history, the glory of America is our ability to come together across the lines that divide us to affirm the ties that bind us. We are one people, we are one nation, we are the United States, and this election will be about coming together, reviving grace, exalting love and making this country be who we say we are: the land for liberty and justice for all. Thank you."

With the speech over, the packed bar descended into a kind of chaos. Some people surged forward to get a picture with the candidate, others were trying to make for the doors. Still others were wondering whether they could get through the crowd to the bathrooms. This time Devin won the selfie scrum. After the speech, not only did she get a picture with Senator Booker, but he recorded a video selfie with her. I was very impressed by Booker's camera work. He took Devin's phone and positioned it so it didn't look like he was a foot taller than Devin, which he was. He had a whole routine:

"Hi, this is Cory Booker with Devin, and I just want to wish everybody at Cedar Falls High School all the best. Get active, get engaged,

Democracy is not a spectator sport. So, please, get out there, make a change. Don't underestimate your power. Use it. Bye bye, now."

Overall, it was a great speech, if a little long, with some soaring language and enough policy to show that he had plans for the Presidency. Julie, who had lived in New Jersey for two years and was already leaning toward Booker, was particularly impressed. We bundled up and headed out onto the arctic vortex landscape, glad we had made the trip.

Chapter 5

Eric Swalwell [3 March 2019]

After driving around much of Iowa to attend events with Presidential candidates, I was looking forward to seeing one close to home. In fact, California U. S. Representative Eric Swalwell wasn't only going to be in Cedar Falls, he was going to be speaking at the home of some good friends and colleagues of mine, Chris and Bettina. So, even though it was one degree out—yes, one (1) lonely degree—I bundled up and drove over with my daughter, Devin, wondering if people would brave the cold and actually show up for this event. When I saw the line of cars in front of the house, I realized that they would. Now that it was officially the beginning of March, Iowans apparently had just decided to ignore bad weather and act as if Spring was on its way. Though, to be honest, there was no sign of this alleged "Spring" coming to Iowa anytime soon during this harsher than normal Winter.

Over the years, I had brought Devin to this very house many times for playdates and sleepovers with Chris and Bettina's daughter, Sabine. The house has a wonderful layout for parties, with a kitchen that opens up into an open great room with a fireplace. In the past, our friends have had big holiday parties here and they've even brought in fellow musicians for pop-up house concerts. So, when we arrived, we knew where to go right away and, still cold, we made a beeline for the front of the fireplace, where David, a friend, had staked out a warm spot. I joined him, and he and I had plenty of time to catch up as I warmed up.

However, this wonderful space also comes with a history. A few years back, a fire that started in their garage spread to their house and could have destroyed the whole home. Fortunately, no one was hurt, but when I went over the next day to help clean up, I saw that the damage was substantial. The great room was charred and burned. Furniture and photographs were destroyed, both on the first floor and in the upstairs back bedroom. Smoke had made its way throughout the whole house. At the time, I wondered whether the house could even be restored.

But if Chris and Bettina shared my doubts, they didn't show it. Almost immediately, they began working with insurance companies and contractors on a multi-year effort to not only restore what had been lost, but to make it better. The room had been nice before, but now it was more open and brighter. In fact, I have to think that having almost lost their house, Chris and Bettina appreciated it even more and felt a kind of karmic obligation to it special events like a candidate visit, for which it was particularly well suited.

All other campaign events that I had attended so far had been with strangers, and while I'm usually not shy about chatting up the person next to me just to pass the time, it was a different thing to attend a house party with people I knew. In fact, I knew the majority of people at this house party. Some were close friends, others I worked with, and still others were recognizable as friends of friends. I found out a lot about how work was going for people and what their kids had been up to. People brought their small children with them, and kids ran around throughout the whole event. In fact, at one point, a toddler brought conversation to a standstill by running into the room and announcing that he had just pooped. We were glad for him. We all would have been happy just to stand around and chat as if this was just another mid-winter party with good friends in a familiar space. It was an added bonus that there happened to be a Presidential candidate speaking.

House party events are very different from rallies. At a rally, there is usually a long, slow-moving line you have to endure to get inside. Then, you spend a long time waiting for things to start, standing in a crowded hall. Some smaller events happen in bars or cafes. At least there, you can get a drink to pass the time. But house parties are different. Hosts are usually thoughtful about putting out a spread, and Iowans, being well trained in potlucks, often pitch in to bring a dish. At this event there was a nice spread of snacks, some of which were even healthy. I thought it was nice of Chris and Bettina to even provide some beer from the local craft brewery.

The other thing that was unique about house parties was that they weren't all about the candidate's speech. Whatever space was to be used for a stage was chosen on the fly, and there wasn't going to be a big production when the candidate arrived. In fact, when Eric Swalwell got to the house, he just made his way through the kitchen like everyone else, stopping in front of the kitchen counter to join one of the conversation clusters. We all kept talking to our friends, and he didn't seem in a hurry to get started. It wasn't like there could be that many rallies to get to on a one-degree day, so the party just continued.

If you watch MSNBC, you have seen Eric Swalwell as a regular guest, and I didn't think twice about engaging him in conversation when he started working the room, as if my seeing him on television was like talking to him on a regular basis in the neighborhood. I've since learned that there is a word for feeling like you actually know someone you've only seen on television: parasocial. I noticed right away that Eric, my parasocial pal, was noticeably younger than me, but I knew I would have to get used to that during this election cycle. Swalwell was glad to chat about the caucus process. I could help but needle the guy from California about coming to Iowa on such a cold day. His district was just east of the San Francisco bay area, so this would have to be outside of his comfort zone. But he wisely wasn't going to complain about the weather, and, in fact, he made a point of mentioning that he was originally from Sac City, Iowa (far from California in many ways). I got to tell him that Sac City had the best nickname ever, "Bag Town."

Eventually, things got started, and Chris took a few minutes to introduce the Representative. Then Swalwell took the "stage," which was really just the sweet spot in front of the fireplace, to start speaking. He stated that when he had graduated school, he had almost $100,000 in debt, which spoke to the concerns of both the millennials in the room and many of the people who work with me at the University of Northern Iowa and want solutions to the student debt crisis.

One thing that stood out in his stump speech was that he foregrounded his support for gun safety legislation, noting that he supported a plan to buy back and ban 15 million assault weapons. He hoped to make that the signature issue that made his campaign stand out from others. He also supported both the Green New Deal and Medicare For All, and his catchphrase for this was "go big, be bold, do good." One illustration of this approach had to do with a unique health research initiative he supported.

"I would propose a trillion-dollar, ten-year Cures in Our Lifetime initiative that would put a next generation of scientists to work, and through genetics, data sharing, and targeted therapies that seek to bring down the cost of health care, extend the quality of life, and create a lot of jobs doing it. I think that would be one way to heal a very divided, a very gridlocked country."

Other highlights from his talk included details from his time as a prosecutor, his support for a journalist protection act, and an argument for a southern border policy not driven by hyped-up "scareavans," groups of migrants that had been dominating news coverage in recent days.

In the Q&A, I got to ask him about the politics of making Medicare For All a reality. He remembered my name from earlier (which I thought was a pretty neat trick), and noted that M4A already was supported by over 50% of the population. No one thought it would be easy to pass, but there was no cause for thinking it was impossible.

When the formal part of the event was over (it wasn't as long as a rally), there was a lot more time for casual chatting. We all still had friends to catch up with, so no one was in a rush to get back out to their cold cars. Devin and her friends were able to speak with the Representative for a while, and they also found Swalwell easy to talk to, though Devin wasn't as sure about what to make about the quaffed campaign photographer who kept angling for pictures (earning that staffer the moniker "Ken doll from the 80s").

The distinctive feature of this event, and the thing which truly made it a house party, was still the toddlers who would occasionally run screaming into the room. Announcements about pooping aside, we all informally agreed to pause our speaking and listening when they crashed the room until they moved on. At one point, this devolved into a chase scene where one of the toddlers was wearing his winter jacket backwards and more-or-less blindly running from his pursuer. This was a sign that it was time to leave before anyone got hurt.

As a U.S. House member, Eric Swalwell had a higher mountain to climb to compete with better-known candidates, but this was how such a journey had to begin, with one conversation and one house party at a time, pausing when the toddlers took over.

Chapter 6
Steve Bullock [5 March 2019]

My decision to see Montana Governor Steve Bullock was made at the last minute. His visit to town came at a busy time for me, and I have to admit that I didn't know much about him. I had to jump onto Wikipedia to find out some details, and I saw that he was a current two-term governor of Montana and chair of the National Governors Association. His national profile might not have been as high as some other candidates, but his credentials were as solid as Bill Clinton's were when he ran for president. So, sure, why shouldn't Governor Bullock dip his toe in to see if he likes the water during an exploratory, pre-announcement trip into town?

That said, my main takeaway from reading Bullock's Wikipedia page was that he and I are the same age. That seemed pertinent because this was the week that the actor Luke Perry (of *Riverdale* and *Beverly Hills 90210* fame) died of a massive stroke. I hadn't realized until reading his obituary that Luke Perry and I were the same age. Now, after reading the Montana governor's Wikipedia page, I saw that he was part of the same club with me and Luke. That all seemed to point toward me going to see him speak.

Okay, the fact that he was speaking at Octopus, my favorite off-campus bar, also made this choice a little easier to make. Octopus is the live music bar on College Hill that is known for its craft beer selection. It also had recently become a watering hole of choice for politicos because of an upcoming special election. A long-serving Democratic state senator in our area unexpectedly stepped down in the middle of his term, setting the stage for an off-cycle contest pitting a Republican former State House member against a Democratic candidate who was currently serving on the Board of Education. Full (and unsurprising) disclosure: the Democratic candidate, Eric Giddens, is a friend and I contributed to his campaign.

All of this mattered because apparently the word had gone out to Presidential candidates that they were welcome to make an appearance to help campaign for Eric. I had to think this announcement was well received by Presidential campaign managers who must have been racking their brains to figure out how to have events that would attract likely Iowa voters in the middle of the worst winter we've had in decades. "Hey, this works!" you could imagine them saying as a light bulb appeared over their heads. Candidates got to speak to a friendly crowd who, if they were going to vote in a state Senate special election in March, were sure to caucus next February. Candidates also would get to show how they would help Iowa rather than just asking for Iowa's help, so politicians had started popping up all over town. It was an interesting wrinkle in the whole process. I mean, even Rachel Maddow name checked Eric, so things were taking a turn for the surreal in this state Senate race.

I also have to think that one of the major differences between this caucus cycle and previous one was how many bars with good beer there were now, and politicians had been gravitating to them like, hmm… what's the right metaphor? Maybe "like college students to beer" would work.

Anyway, I got to Octopus and ordered a delicious sour as Steve Bullock and his entourage got settled in. We were surrounded by college students with beer, so I guess that metaphor worked. Octopus is not a huge bar, so basically we all sat around chatting in conversation clusters while the Governor worked the room and Eric talked to people about his State Senate campaign.

I hung out with a colleague, Theresa, and it turned out we both had an interest in hybrids and electric cars. I get that this confirms basically every stereotype about my being an English professor, so I might as well fess up now and embrace my stereotype. Yes, I now have an electric car; yes, I am tempted to correct the errors in your text messages; yes, I know how to use a semicolon. There you go. Come at me!

There was a small but respectable crowd by the time Eric took to the stage to say a little bit about his campaign and then to introduce Steve Bullock. I live posted the first few minutes of Bullock's speech, and then I expected to sit back and listen to the rest of what he had to say. But I had captured almost his entire speech. I guess because this wasn't a regular campaign event, it was considered bad form to give a 20-minute talk. Alas, this was when I also learned that Facebook Live only saved posts for a little while, so I don't have any direct quotes from the Governor's remarks.

He was running in the moderate lane, but he was eager to promote win-win policies that had popular support. Though not a supporter of the Green New Deal, per se, he argued that investments in alternative energy would have a multiplier effect. Yes, they would reduce greenhouse gas emissions, but they would also create new jobs and have the effect of lowering the cost of energy. Such measures would prove popular in wide swaths of the country.

The abbreviated stump speech was enough time to get a sense of where Bullock stood and why he wanted to run. Though there were policy differences separating the candidates I'd seen so far, the main difference between them was strategic, and the strategy mattered a lot to voters. Basically, it came down to how to run against Trump. Was the best approach to expand the base by appealing to young and other infrequent voters? Or was the key to bring back one-time Obama supporters who voted for Trump in 2016? Or, was this a false choice, and was it possible to do both things at the same time? Sure, that final option sound great, but if you tried to do both things at that same time, would you squander resources and risk losing? These remained difficult questions to answer in advance, but they were the kind of things that haunted campaigns. In retrospect, they look like easy decisions (i.e. "why didn't Hillary campaign in Wisconsin?"), but there was nothing easy about them in the moment.

Governor Bullock was clearly on the side of bringing Trump voters into the fold. And, fair enough, that was his wheelhouse. He was the governor of a red state and won re-election by four points at the same time that Trump took the state by over 20. In a state like Iowa with a large rural population and more than its fair share of Obama/Trump voters, it was an argument that may have some merit.

But really, the whole speech didn't take more than five minutes and then we were back to our conversation clusters. The governor began working the room, starting with a group of college students near the stage. At that moment, when I saw a sitting governor struggle to lure reluctant undergraduates into participating in a discussion, I fully felt his pain. It ain't easy.

Eventually, Bullock made his way over to where Theresa and I were standing. We talked a little bit about the campaign, and he came across as a very personable guy who was not at all uncomfortable chatting up a room of strangers. I informed him about my discovery that he and I and Luke Perry were all the same age. The governor did not seem particularly impressed by this information, though it later occurred to me that he may simply not have known who Luke Perry was.

When the conversation moved to energy policy, he was on steadier ground. As noted earlier, he was eager to embrace renewable resources both for tackling climate change and because it was becoming more and more economically feasible to do so. I decided to throw him a tougher question, channeling my inner Chuck Todd. I pointed out that once the easier-but-by-no-means guaranteed solutions like maximizing renewable energy are done, the remaining sources of greenhouse emissions are harder to tackle.

"For example," I asked, "What about methane?"

"Methane?" he asked, looking puzzled. "You mean, like, cattle?"

Methane, from cattle as well as other sources like natural gas leaks, is responsible for about one quarter of greenhouse gas emissions, so, yeah, like, cattle.

The governor wasn't going to go there with me, and he implied that until you had people on board with renewable energy, you would only scare off potential supporters by even discussing something like this. And, fair enough, I didn't expect the governor of a cattle state like Montana to announce a campaign to reduce beef consumption at a bar in Iowa. Still, it would at least have been nice to see that he'd given the subject some thought. But no. We talked a little while more and then he moved on. Pretty soon the bar started to empty out. When the governor left I realized that his entourage included all the best haircuts in the bar.

I left hoping that maybe my conversation would cause the governor to do some research on methane emissions and to think about how to tackle some of the thornier issues surrounding global warming. But, realistically, probably the most I could hope for is that he would look at Luke Perry's Wikipedia page.

Chapter 7

Beto O'Rourke [16 March 2019]

Sometimes it took candidates a little while to make it to our northeastern corner of Iowa, but Beto O'Rourke, the former U. S. Representative from El Paso, Texas, announced he was coming to Waterloo just a couple of days after he declared that he was running for President. The draw was the special election for a State Senate seat here that I wrote about in the last chapter. This was the weekend before the election, and candidates were lining up to drum up support for Eric Giddens in his race for office. In addition to O'Rourke, Amy Klobuchar, John Delaney, and Cory Booker were going to be visiting within a day and a half. Whoa! That was too much even for me. Just Beto for now.

My son, Nic, was back for Spring Break, and he and my daughter, Devin, were up for the event. I pulled up the event advertisement on my phone and saw that it was scheduled for the county Party headquarters in Waterloo, a room that fit 50 people at most. 150 had already RSVPed to the Facebook invite. As I plugged my phone in to make sure it was fully charged, I wondered how this would all work.

I was too clever for my own good. On our way into downtown Waterloo, I realized that I had left my phone charging at home, and I didn't have time to go back for it. Fortunately, as sweet as Devin is, she said I could use her phone during the event (she was 17, so this was a big sacrifice) as long as I gave it back to her at the end so she could get a picture with Beto.

Crisis averted. However, Devin, who also is devoted in her efforts to learn Spanish, has set her phone so that all the instructions are *en Español*. I have been less devoted in my efforts, and I soon realized that I was going to have to muddle through while determining whether I wanted to *listo* or *cancelar* a picture.

It was a nice, early Spring day, and the campaign had wisely decided to have the event outside in a parking lot adjacent to party headquarters. There was a decent sized crowd, even more in attendance than those who had RSVPed. However, having the event in the parking lot meant that we were sharing the lot with a portable giant cow statue, which everyone seemingly agreed to ignore. Fair enough, as the cow (whose butt was facing the crowd) also ignored us.

At the event, the first person we saw was Arlo, a friend whom our kids had grown up with and known forever. He was also back on Spring Break, and when we caught up to him he was signing up to canvas for Eric Giddens following the event. We were also on board, and we signed out a clipboard so we could knock on doors after the rally.

I confess that I wasn't quite sure about this location as the backdrop for a big event, giant cow butt aside. It was better than trying to have a rally inside, in a space that would have been too small for the crowd, but this was just a parking lot next to an old brick building, and the stage was just somebody's pick-up truck parked in front of the brick wall. I grew even less sure when the candidate's car drove up, and the initial photos I took had a porta-potty and a rickety staircase in the background.

But, fortunately, none of that made a difference. O'Rourke slowly made his way through the crowd to the bed of the pickup and took the stage (the flatbed?) to chants of "Beto! Beto!" I appreciated that he was wearing a University of Northern Iowa cap for the occasion. After being introduced, Beto was charged up, and he worked the crowd from the get go.

"How's everybody doing? It is so good to be with you on such a beautiful day. Waterloo and El Paso, Texas, have just traded weather systems. It's snowing in my hometown right now, as we speak, and it could not be more gorgeous than it is right now here, with all of you."

O'Rourke was an energetic speaker. As had been noted by He-Who-Shall-Not-Be-Named, Beto talked with his hands, and in one picture I took he looked more like a conductor than a candidate. My wife, Julie, was at home, but she realized that this event was being televised live on MSNBC, and she sent a message that popped up on Devin's phone (or, at least that was what I assumed when an alert appeared that was titled *Mensajes—ahora*).

This event was more about politics than policy, and his aim in whipping up the crowd was to persuade people to get more involved in the process. It was preaching to the choir, but an event like this was choir rehearsal. That said, one issue that had been recently in the news was the separation of parents from children at the southern border with Mexico, and O'Rourke did not hold anything back in his condemnation of this action.

"We must ensure that we never again take children, at their most desperate and vulnerable moment, from their parents after they have travelled 2,000 miles, leaving some of the most violent countries in the world, deporting those parents back to the countries from which they fled in the first place, and locking those kids up in cages, or can we be the country that decides those asylum seekers who can find a home here, they will be better for it, but so will this country?"

Wow, now that I type it up, I see that that was one crazy sentence, and I'm still not sure I punctuated it right. But in the moment, delivered with Beto's pulsating cadence, it was a big applause line.

O'Rourke also took a clear side in the main strategy debate over whether Democrats needed to expand the base or appeal to working-class voters lost to Trump in the last election. Beto's side was "both," and there was a case to be made that an inspiring candidacy could win all kinds of voters (as Obama did in 2008). But there was also a risk that trying to be all things to all people could lead to less ambitious policy proposals. Again, this was not a policy speech by any means, so it would not have been quite fair to be looking for a white paper on monetary policy. The main reason Beto was here was to rally voters for Eric Giddens, and he did a great job at that.

The normally-empty parking lot with the giant cow statue happened to be a block away from the county courthouse, where early voting was happening, and O'Rourke encouraged people to both vote and then to canvas on behalf of Eric, before turning the pick-up truck over to Eric. That was when I realized Beto had a loud voice and was able to out-shout a rowdy crowd. Eric was more soft-spoken, and fortunately Beto was able to hand him an electronic megaphone. Though I had earlier wondered about the appropriateness of this backdrop, when photos of the event were published, they looked great. It was a sunny day, and the brick wall gave the whole scene a rugged, almost edgy vibe, even without the giant cow statue.

When Beto finished speaking, Devin demanded her phone back and joined the crowd, hoping for a picture. Nic, having learned an important lesson at an earlier event with Kirstin Gillibrand, positioned himself between the candidate and his getaway car. I ended up jammed in, unable to get closer to the candidate or to leave, and now I was without a phone. So, I eavesdropped.

What I heard was interesting, and depending on your opinion, was either endearing or obnoxious. Apparently, Iowans were willing to wait a long time in a big crowd, getting pushed and crushed, in order to get their chance to speak to the candidate. However, once they got there, what did they want to do? They wanted to give unsolicited campaign advice. One woman fought her way through the scrum to tell O'Rourke that he should run on a ticket with Eric Swalwell as his vice president. Another guy was willing to wait an extra 20 minutes to offer the candidate a campaign slogan (which was something innocuous like "Together We Rise"). Having performed this function as unpaid advisors, these people were happy. All of this reminded me of people bringing mitts to pro baseball games in hopes of catching a foul ball.

Devin and Nic were able to get pictures, and afterward we walked the block to the county courthouse so that Nic and Arlo could cast their votes for Eric (they would both be back at college when the election happened). The only laugh line from that excursion was when I forgot to take my harmonica out of my pocket and got buzzed by the metal detector. But then we were off to canvas, and among the people who were home, there was a surprising level of awareness of this snap special election. It was not clear what role all the visiting Presidential candidates played in this,

but it couldn't have hurt to be in the national spotlight for a while. Happily, three days later, Eric Giddens won a decisive, double-digit percentage victory in the Special Election. *Sí, se puede!*

Chapter 8

Pete Buttigieg [17 April 2019]

On his initial swing through Iowa after announcing his campaign for President, South Bend, Indiana, mayor Pete Buttigieg only got as close to us as Marshalltown, a 45-minute drive from home. I had already driven there once to see a Cory Booker event, and that was in even worse weather, so, okay, Mayor Pete, I would make the trip to see you at a house party. Besides, this would be my opportunity to learn to spell "Buttigieg."

Buttigieg had made a pretty big initial splash, and I wondered whether the house party format would work for him. Such gatherings are usually small events held in a supporter's living room, and I had to think there would be more people in attendance than the average living room could hold. As I made my way to Marshalltown and approached the destination, in a neighborhood of modest-sized houses with cars lined up around the block, I thought this was going to be interesting. Then I got to the house and things got interesting in a way I hadn't anticipated.

Apparently, a right-wing homophobic group had decided to stalk and disrupt all of Buttigieg's events. Parked right in front of the house was an expensive tour bus covered with Biblical verses. Basically, it looked like a Dr. Bronner's bottle with wheels. Out in front of the bus, there was a guy wearing a devil costume shouting over a loudspeaker. He was accompanied by a guy in a Jesus costume with running shoes who was dragging a giant cross. To get to the house, we had to walk in front of Satan and Jesus's Jay and Silent Bob routine. Of course, this whole schtick was meant to be visually arresting, so on principle I'm not going to reproduce any pictures of it here. You'll have to make due with vicious mockery.

Once I got past the clown show, I saw that the organizers had wisely abandoned the house party model and relocated the event to the backyard, where people gathered around a deck. The Devil had about a three minute quasi-comedy routine with lines like "leave your baptismal vows at the door" that he kept repeating. It was like listening to Dennis Miller on an infinite loop, so in that regard it may have been an accurate rendition of Hell.

Fortunately, I ran into some friends, Christine and Del, from town. Christine works with the National Breast Cancer Coalition and is an omnipresent force within our area on issues related to advocacy around breast cancer-related issues. The three of us got to catch up and chat about Buttigieg, the weather, and basically anything else that allowed us to block out the sound of the droning Devil.

Buttigieg made for an interesting political figure because of how he checked a series of boxes that made him difficult to pigeonhole. He was a mayor of a modest-sized city, he was openly gay, he was a veteran, at 37 he was the youngest candidate in the race, he was running as more of a moderate than most other candidates I had seen so far, he wore his intellect on his sleeve, and his vibe fit clearly within a soft-spoken midwestern type. That's quite a list, and all of it made for a compelling, and complex, story.

People continued filling in the backyard, and event organizers began fiddling with a public address system, which clearly had been set up at the last minute and was not working. Meanwhile, Satan's sound system was pretty robust, and he had relocated to the alley next to the backyard. He was only about 30 yards from where Buttigieg was to speak, belting out quasi-hymns and retelling the same lame jokes. There was one good moment when the Devil stopped singing in the middle of a hymn to answer his phone. Then the Devil started texting.

As the scheduled start time for the event came and went, about 150 people crowded into the backyard. The crowd began chanting "Boot-edge-edge" (I had thought the pronunciation was "Buddha-judge," but whatever) to drown out the Devil. When organizers parked cars in the backyard, blocking Satan's sight line, we all cheered. But that got old after a while, and soon even the Devil seemed bored. An organizer stood up on the deck and clearly lied to us by announcing "he's almost here."

Conversation turned surreal, as often happens when events run late. A guy standing next to me started telling a story about his high school in North Dakota, which had "the Satans" as their mascot. He said it was weird to go to basketball games and hear a gym full of people shouting "go, Satans!" Then, four different people began working on the sound system, which gave me some hope that the event would actually take place. About five minutes later, there was the sound of a pop and buzz, and it looked like we were a go.

Soon after, Pete Buttigieg took to the deck to the applause of the crowd and the sound of mock whispering from Satan. Buttigieg and the crowd made an implicit, unspoken agreement to ignore the protesting duo and proceed as if they weren't there. Mayor Pete thanked everyone for coming out, and acknowledged that this crowd was never going to fit into a living room for an inside-the-house party, stating "as you have seen this thing has taken off a little bit faster than even we could have guessed."

That was an applause line for the crowd whose presence made the event big. Though we were outside, Buttigieg said he was going to stick with the house party model and go with a short talk with lots of time for questions. He introduced both his husband and his mom, both of whom were here for the event, and that was very sweet. Even the Devil let that one pass without comment.

In his stump speech, Buttigieg alternated between a big picture vision and a wonkish interest in policy details. He spoke about global warming in terms of climate security, but he was also happy to go down a rabbit hole detailing regulations to ensure local drinking water safety. When he spoke about the federal deficit, he described it as a generational issue, and when discussing challenges facing the fundamental principles of Democracy, his reference point was clear to the crowd.

Much of his vision was an argument for common sense approaches. For example, "It would help if we had an EPA head who supported the environment." These were easy applause lines, and they drew on shared frustration with an administration willing to ignore basic science and burn down decades of incremental progress on issues. Mayor Pete discussed decriminalization and legalization of marijuana as non-emotional policy matters to be worked out. However, there was a cautiousness in Buttigieg's rhetoric that spoke to a tendency to hedge his bets. At one point, he announced that he supported "Medicare for all who want it," which sounded good but meant he didn't support Medicare for All. "Medicare for all who want it" was more like a public option within Obamacare, which was better than what we have now but something less than an ambitious overhaul of the public health care system. To be fair, he did talk about a "glide path" toward Medicare for All, but how that would all happen was not clear.

My friend Christine got to ask him a question, and requested his support for a platform in support of breast cancer research and health care access. Mayor Pete said he looked forward to reviewing that platform and supported the general principles. This was a personal issue for him, as he had recently lost his father to cancer and was aware of the challenges that many families faced.

Reflecting on that time, he noted, "One of the things that struck me was that for all the challenges we faced, we had also the benefit of the freedom to focus on what was right for our family because we did not have to focus on whether it was going to bankrupt us, thanks to Medicare. And it was a reminder about the freedom that is created through the right kind of policies."

I kept in touch with Christine about this issue. About a week later, the campaign sent an email stating that Buttigieg would sign onto the NBCC Policy Platform, but when I made my initial blog post about this event, he hadn't done so officially, and I had to note that. However, that proved a good excuse for a round of email exchanges, and soon after I was able to confirm that some harried campaign workers were able to make it official that Pete Buttigieg signed on as the ninth candidate to support the NBCC Policy Platform.

After Buttigieg finished speaking, there was a rush to the deck for pictures. It was pretty hard to compete with the little girls who drew pictures and made cookies for the event, so I wasn't able to get very close to the candidate. Overall, Buttigieg did a nice job mixing inspirational

messages with policy details that focused on common sense (rather than cutting edge) solutions. He left the crowd in a good mood, and it was easy to feel sympathy for a candidate who has to deal with homophobic trolls in costumes.

By the time I left, Satan had slithered away quietly and was nowhere to be seen.

Chapter 9

Amy Klobuchar [25 May 2019]

I had missed an opportunity to see Minnesota Senator Amy Klobuchar closer to home, so I did not mind driving up to Decorah for this event. Decorah is a beautiful little town tucked in the very northeast corner of Iowa not far from the Minnesota border. Besides, she was scheduled to speak at a place called the Lingonberry, which sounded like somewhere I might be able to get a good cup of coffee and perhaps one of those Norwegian pastries.

It took me a little longer to get to Decorah than I had planned, and then a farmer's market was happening in the lot where I thought I could park, so by the time I got to the Lingonberry, along the picturesque main drag in Decorah, it was almost the official start time. All the seats were taken in a bare, brick lined room that seemed to have no other apparent purpose than hosting presidential candidates. I wasn't going to be getting coffee and a pastry, but I was able to stand right near the makeshift stage.

The crowd was probably around 150, which was good for a Saturday morning in a small town, but it wasn't the most diverse group I've seen. Almost everyone was white, middle-aged or retired, and relatively affluent (to the extent I could read such qualities off of clothing and haircuts). I don't know if this was a reflection of Klobuchar's appeal or just the demographics of Decorah. However, I should note that the crowd did include one millennial studiously reading a David Sedaris book and ignoring everything around her.

Everyone was on good behavior. The most exciting thing that happened in the run up to the event was that one of the "Amy" signs fell off the wall. While three staffers ran up to retape it, people in the audience shouted out adhesive suggestions. When the sign was reattached to the wall, there was applause. It was an "Iowa nice" crowd.

We were prepped by a local official who noted he lived so close to Minnesota that he could see it from his deck. He also informed us that it was the Senator's birthday, so when she arrived pretty close to on time, we all sang "Happy Birthday," and I got to shake her hand on her way in. Klobuchar began on a light note, joking about the time she was introduced as "Minnesota's senior citizen" instead of senior Senator. She also milked the Minnesota/Iowa connection for all it was worth, telling stories to an appreciative audience about meeting the King of Norway, about announcing her campaign in the middle of a snowstorm, and offering a shout out to former Iowa Senator Tom Harkin. She also had family in tow, with her husband and daughter in attendance.

Of course, there was policy as well. Klobuchar knows her issues and can get into the nuts and bolts of legislation that she wants to pass. She spoke a fair amount about education and agricultural policy (she's on the Senate Agriculture Committee and worried specifically about the awful rise in the rural suicide rate). She noted that on day one of a Klobuchar administration the U. S. would rejoin the Paris climate accords. On day two she would restore Obama era pollution controls.

That said, her agenda was not the most ambitious I had heard on the campaign trail. She supported allowing for student loan debt to be refinanced at a lower rate, as well as for expanding Pell Grants, but she did not go as far as the free college tuition plans that other candidates, such as Sanders and Warren, had endorsed. Similarly, she supported a public health care option within Obamacare but not Medicare for All. Klobuchar's emphasis, as she stated, was "getting things done" and focusing on "bread and butter issues." As a midwestern candidate, she made a case very similar to Pete Buttigeig's about her ability to win back states that had flipped to Trump, and argued that she could be competitive in non-Democratic areas.

"So, I have always, through my life—and maybe it's because of my background—I've been blunt, I tell people the truth, and I then build trust. And I've done that...in every county in Minnesota every single year—there's 87 of them and I visit them all every single year— and I have gone to the most reddest of Republican counties, where people didn't agree with me on everything, but we find common ground on things that matter to them."

One of her stronger moments was when she spoke about immigration reform, building a mini-stemwinder that got an enthusiastic response from the crowd.

"We also need immigration reform. Because the way I look at it, when you've got 70 of our Fortune 500 companies that have been headed up by people from other countries (true fact), when you've got 25% of our U.S. Nobel laureates—our United States Nobel laureates—were born in other countries before they won those Nobel laureates. Immigrants don't diminish America. They are America."

The one surprise of her talk was an anecdote she only recently had begun sharing involving the late Senator John McCain. Apparently, she sat between Senators John McCain and Bernie Sanders at Trump's inauguration speech, the one that George W. Bush reportedly described as "weird shit" (Bush's description, not Klobuchar's). While President Trump spoke, Senator McCain began listing the names of various dictators under his breath while listening to Trump's now-infamous recitation of "American carnage."

Overall, Klobuchar gave an upbeat, forward-looking speech, and the only time a little edge emerged was during the question-and-answer session when an ACLU member was called on and pulled out a pre-written question while a friend fumbled with a phone to record it. The Senator was a little piqued to have to stand there waiting just to be called out on the carpet. The question had to do with the number of detained persons at the Southern border and whether Klobuchar would pledge to a specific number of reduced imprisonments. She would not commit to a specific number, though, of course, she did not support Trump's detention policy or anything he was doing at the Southern border.

The questions ranged from notably informed to pretty crackpot. A member of a local climate group wanted her to commit to a carbon tax. She said it was "one of the things we can look at." I was impressed that in response to a question about mental health care, she was able to reference Iowa's particularly bad situation, with only 64 beds for residential mental health care in the whole state. Someone else asked her a question she hadn't heard before about whether she worried Trump would not support the peaceful transition of power if he lost re-election (you might remember Michael Cohen making such a claim during his Congressional testimony). This provoked some nervous laughter in the crowd. Klobuchar wasn't going to encourage any conspiratorial thinking, but she did say that she worried about a close election and supported backup paper ballots for all elections.

And then, if you can believe it, one guy had the gall to suggest that instead of running for President, she should run as Pete Buttigieg's vice president! Wow, that let me see how quickly an "Iowa nice" crowd could turn ugly. People booed the guy and began heckling him. I wondered if someone might drag him out into an alley and rough him up. Well, okay, it was still Iowa. Maybe someone would drag him out into an alley and have a heartfelt conversation about manners and how we treat our guests. Actually, Klobuchar handled this moment really smoothly. She was not at all thrown off and had a good comeback about how she supported having lots of candidates in the race, saying, "may the best woman win."

When the event was over, I happened to be right next to where Klobuchar was greeting people. There was a sweet moment where a dad brought some "Amy" campaign signs up for her signature so he could give them to his daughters. I got to wish her "Happy Birthday" before my picture was taken with her. As I left the Lingonberry, it was a beautiful, early summer day in an idyllic small town. Plenty of people were wandering the downtown strip, moving in and out stores and sharing warm greetings. I found a nearby coffee shop and was able to buy my long-deferred pastry. It was worth the trip.

Chapter 10
Bernie Sanders [8 June 2019]

It was a warm summer day, and Bernie Sanders was going to be speaking in Waterloo, the next town over from where I live, at a location that is accessible by bike trail. I thought I'd do something unusual and bike there. Of course, when I read the online event description, I saw that parking was limited and they were encouraging people to bike. So, maybe my idea was not so novel.

The event was taking place at the National Cattle Congress, a long-standing fairground and event center that must have been established when this part of Iowa did more cattle farming than it does now. Now, it is known primarily for a yearly exhibition/carnival held in the fall and for cheap event space to rent for the rest of the year.

When I got to the building where Bernie's event was taking place, there was no place to lock up my bike. I cruised the parking lot in search of a bike rack, but all I found was that the Iowa high school rodeo was also taking place on the premises. I wondered if there might be anyone attending both events. Eventually, I had to lock up my bike on a downspout, but it was right next to a police car, which I think is always the best place to park when you're not sure if you've got a legit spot for your bike.

So, Bernie. Full disclosure: I caucused for Bernie in 2016, and at this point in the process I knew that I might support him again. I was remaining uncommitted in the spirit of this project, but I was also remaining uncommitted because I actually wasn't sure. I had generally found something to like in every person I had seen speak, though I had my own policy preferences which tilted me more toward some candidates than others. Like most people who viewed defeating Donald Trump as the existential point of this whole process, I was looking for a candidate who was equipped to do that, and that might have been Bernie. I was looking forward to seeing him speak, even though I had gone to several of his events during the last campaign. As far as Iowa was concerned, Bernie was the OG of the field.

There was already a pretty good crowd by the time I arrived at the event hall. The hall itself had the worn feel of the kind of place one would go to either for estate auctions or punk rock shows. In fact, the crowd looked pretty evenly split between people who attended estate auctions and people who attended punk rock shows. I saw a staffer ask someone if she wanted to be on stage behind Bernie. My ears perked up, as I'd learned to be shameless about such opportunities. I caught the staffer's eye, and she asked if I wanted to be on stage. Yes, please. She glanced at my bicycling outfit and deemed the colorful RAGBRAI shirt "too busy." She said I would have to be in a back row on the stage. I was good with that, so I was given a Golden Ticket. Well, actually, it was just a blue wristband, but it was still going to get me into Willy Wonka's Chocolate Factory.

Meanwhile, Julie and Devin showed up, along with some friends who were visiting for the weekend to take in some candidate events. They had been in Des Moines earlier that day to see presidential candidates at the Pride festival where, in one of the best moments ever caught on camera, Devin had pestered Bernie to get a picture with him. I had thought they all would have had their fill of candidates after the Pride fest, but no, they were up for more, and I was going to have company up on stage.

Once it came time to take our places, we were given strict instructions not to be on our phones during the speech. Having given such instructions many times to students, I felt an obligation to follow this rule. Instead we were given signs to wave as needed. However, I was able to take a quick picture of Bernie's water bottle, which I knew was his because it said "Bernie" in big letters.

Things weren't running too late by the time it all got started. There were about 300 people in the attendance, which was pretty impressive, and it had the feel of one of the big-turnout events in the run up to the 2016 caucus. There were a couple opening speakers to get the crowd whipped up, and then Bernie took the stage to a loud ovation from the crowd and plenty of sign waving from those of us on the stage behind him. One downside of being on the stage was that all we got to see was the back of Bernie's head, and it looked like he had gotten a sunburn earlier in the day on his bald spot. Bernie, use sunscreen!

Following the rules I had agreed to, I didn't take my phone out when Bernie was speaking, so I didn't get to record any of what he said, but that was not really necessary because he had been saying the same things for 30 years. I know that sounds like a dig, but it is not intended as one. One of the things that distinguished Bernie was his consistency. He was always on message, and it was a message about economic inequality and what the government can do to both mitigate and reverse it by challenging the powers that be.

"We're going to have to take them all on. We're talking about Wall Street, we're talking about the fossil fuel industry and the insurance companies and the drug companies and the military industrial complex and the corporate media, all the power that is out there trying to preserve the status quo."

So, it was not a surprise to hear him zero in on how much of the nation's wealth was controlled by a small number of families. The Walton family (of Wal-Mart) were particularly in his sights on this night because he had recently spoken at the Wal-Mart shareholders meeting on behalf of low wage workers and called for the company to raise its minimum wage to $15 an hour. During that meeting he had said, "Despite the incredible wealth of its owner, Walmart pays many of its employees starvation wages, wages that are so low that many of these employees are forced to rely on government programs like food stamps, Medicaid and public housing in order to survive." It was easy to encapsulate the issue of income inequality when you realize that the Walton family, as Bernie often said, "owns more wealth than the bottom 40 percent of the American people," a claim that Politifact checked out and flagged as "true."

There also were plenty of applause lines when he targeted big pharma and student loan debt. It was a pretty raucous crowd, and I saw Bernie do something I hadn't seen him do before in a speech. He shouted out to the crowd asking if people knew what the interest rates were if they took out a payday loan. There were a number of people with anecdotes to share about payday lenders, and Bernie riffed off of their stories. It was more back and forth than you usually see with a big crowd like that.

In the end, I had thought there would be some Q&A, but Bernie was in barnburner mode, and it ended up just being a speech that laid out the task ahead, the forces that had to be confronted, and the stakes we all faced. "Maybe instead of spending a trillion and a half dollars every year on weapons designed to kill other people, maybe we should invest in transforming our energy system and saving the planet for our children and grandchildren."

There was no pretending that things were going to be easy, and in this regard it wasn't the most uplifting speech. This was more a "let's get ready to rumble" call out to Bernie's people. They were ready for him. Unlike the last campaign, Bernie now seemed to have fully given himself over to selfies. When the speech was over, the true advantage of being on stage behind him became clear. We lined up for a moment with the candidate and got spots toward the front of the crowd. As I passed on my phone to a staffer and stood next to Bernie, I thanked him for coming and said he had had a long day. For the record, he spoke at the Pride festival in Des Moines, had a town hall event in Marshalltown, and then this event in Waterloo. It would have been exhausting just to attend all of those things in one day, never mind being the speaker. Bernie gave me a brief nod in agreement. "It was a long day," he said, "but a great day."

Chapter 11

Bill de Blasio [6 June 2019]

The announcement came late for a "Breakfast with Bill" event featuring New York City mayor Bill de Blasio. That seemed par for the course since de Blasio was also the last person with a national profile to announce that he was running for the Presidency. This breakfast event was happening during a weekend when candidates were swarming the state. I had seen Bernie Sanders the night before, and I was already planning to see John Hickenlooper and Kamala Harris later that day, but my morning was open. Besides, we were told "breakfast is provided," and the event was slated for Newton's, a favorite cafe in downtown Waterloo.

We still had out-of-town guests visiting, and a couple of them, along with my daughter Devin, were also up for "Breakfast with Bill," so we made an early start of it and were able to get seats at a table on the outdoor patio where the meet-and-greet was slated to happen. It was a nice idea to be outside and under an awning on a warm, sunny morning in June. There were about 50 people there, a crowd of usual suspects, party officials and local activists I mostly recognized from other events, including my friend Christine, who worked with the National Breast Cancer Coalition and whom I had hung out with at a Pete Buttigieg event. These were reliable people who could be counted on to turn out. However, the cafe also had a number of people who were just there for breakfast and seemed to be confused as to why it was so crowded. I had thought maybe a buffet would be set up for those of us here for the event, but there wasn't anything, and it didn't look like there were any additional staff working. I began to have my doubts about breakfast.

Soon enough, Mayor de Blasio arrived and began working the crowd. The first thing I noticed was how tall he is. Afterward, I looked it up on Wikipedia and found out that he is 6' 5"—though Wikipedia packaged that info in an utterly meaningless factoid: "At a height of 6 ft 5 in (1.96 m), de Blasio is the tallest mayor in New York City history." He was there with his notably shorter wife, Chirlane McCray (whose height was not available online).

When de Blasio came over to our table, we all shook his hand and chatted amiably. One of our guests was originally from Yonkers, New York, and I felt obligated to bring this up, considering how close it was to New York City. de Blasio nodded and said something about this being a long way to come. He then moved on to shake more hands and immediately spoke with a guy who said he was from Brooklyn. I could see that it was not going to be that surprising to find former New Yorkers in Iowa. Of course, since my wife, Julie, is originally from Rochester, New York, I probably should have realized that already.

After working the crowd a bit, the formal part of the event got started, and I could see that there was no hope for even a cup of coffee. But I marshalled on as the Waterloo mayor welcomed the New York City mayor and his wife. Chirlane McCray spoke first. She had been an activist and spoke about her work as a mental health advocate. Then she turned the stage over to her husband.

When de Blasio took the stage, he started with a nice set piece about how he and McCray had first met when they were working at city hall together. She had come over to his desk to ask for something. "I looked up from my desk and I saw her gliding like an angel toward me. And I guarantee you all, I experienced something like love at first sight. It actually exists: love at first sight. And Chirlane McCray experienced absolutely nothing." However, perseverance paid off, and he eventually won her over. He also spoke about the challenges they both faced in caring for elderly parents.

After the personal opening, de Blasio turned to policy, detailing his work as mayor in New York City, focusing on programs and reforms aimed at improving the quality of life for working New Yorkers. During his administration the city had begun free universal pre-K and school lunches, and much of his speech was about the impact of income inequality on issues like health care access. Having just seen Bernie Sanders speak the night before, I was surprised to see him echoing many of the same themes. de Blasio was running in the same lane, which I suppose I should have realized.

It is worth noting that de Blasio's campaign had not been received well by New Yorkers. Surveys showed that most of his constituents who were asked did not want him to run for President. However, my past experience with New Yorkers made me take such polls with a grain of salt. In New York City, dislike was a form of affection. To be truly unpopular in the City, one had to be ignored.

Toward the end of his stump speech, de Blasio zeroed in on Trump, calling him a schoolyard bully and the "con-mander in chief," and the Mayor argued that it was important to stand up to and confront a schoolyard bully, who would back down when intimidation didn't work. de Blasio illustrated this theory with an example related to immigration.

"He threatened us, early in his administration with an executive order on immigration. And I want to tell you, he threatened to take away security funding from New York—as a New Yorker—he was going to take away security funding from New York. New York City—and I'm sorry to say this, but it's true—is the number one terrorism target in the United States of America. We know this from painful experience. The President of the United States threatened to take away security funding unless we asked immigrants their documentation status. And I said 'I'm not doing that." and my police commissioner said 'I'm not doing that,' because we knew if we started asking every immigrant their documentation status no immigrant who was undocumented would ever report a crime again. They would never come forward as a witness. We needed cooperation between our police and community. We've proven it works. We're the safest big city in America right now. So we said 'no' to Donald Trump. We said 'no.' We said, we are not changing who we are and our values. We will not make our city less safe because you are trying to intimidate us. Now, we said something very simple, and I said it out loud. 'What you are doing on immigration to do is unconstitutional. We will go to court and we will beat you in court.' And we proceeded to beat him in court."

Lesson learned.

In the Q&A, de Blasio talked about efforts to address climate change, and he mentioned the creation of a network of charging stations for electric vehicles in New York City. As a new electric car owner, this caught my attention. Since I was standing right next to the Waterloo mayor, I took the opportunity to lean over and put in a plug (sorry, I know that's a bad pun, but that's what I said at the time without realizing it). I mentioned that there was no electric car charging station in downtown Waterloo. Without missing a beat, the mayor replied, "And there's no money for one either." Zing! I took this as a personal challenge to search out some grant money or other type of funding, and I made a few phone calls afterward with little success. However, about six months later, a public electric car charger was unveiled in downtown Waterloo, and I am glad to be a regular user of it.

After the Q&A, de Blasio and McCray were available for pictures, a moment I did not let slip by, as Devin and I were able to get shots with both of them. Though when the mayor towered over me, it became even more evident how tall he really is. My friend Christine, who went through a lot of rigamarole to get Pete Buttigieg to sign onto the NBCC Policy Platform, had a much easier time with Bill de Blasio. When she explained the platform, he had someone hand him a pen, and he gave the platform his John Hancock on the spot.

Soon the event began breaking up, and we didn't stick around, since we still needed to eat breakfast. It was the beginning of a day when I would be attending three candidates events. I needed to be well fortified.

Chapter 12

John Hickenlooper [6 June 2019]

I approached the "Have a Beer with John Hickenlooper" event with some caution, since this very morning I had attended a "Breakfast with Bill de Blasio" at which I did not have breakfast. John Hickenlooper was the governor of Colorado, and before his political career began he ran a very successful brewing company in Denver, so it made sense that he would be having a meet-and-greet at a Cedar Rapids brewpub. I had to hope there would actually be beer involved.

When I arrived, I could see right away that this event had a good set up. Tables were stationed at the door, and no one was getting in without being asked to sign in. Additionally, the benefit of signing in was that you got a ticket for a beer and a beer cozy (or is it koozie?). I have never in my life found a good reason to use a beer cozy. If you are nursing your beer so long that it gets warm, you should have ordered something different. But I was happy to take the ticket and order one of the house specialties, a dark sour beer, which tasted a little thin at first but then grew on me.

This particular brew pub was the Quarter Barrel Arcade and Brewery, and the bar was faced by a row of classic pinball machines, mostly from the 1980s, a period during which I had misspent a fair share of my youth and early adulthood playing pinball. So, with beer in hand and quarters in my pocket, I had to say that I felt I had been demographically pretty well targeted for this event. I put my money into the *Ghostbusters* machine before I noticed that it had already been loaded up with credits. But after a warm up game (in which I got a credit on match), I played again and tore the machine up with a long multiball session. In fact, I missed Hickenlooper's entrance because I was doing so well.

But that was okay because the Governor had decided to work the room before the formal part of the event began. When I finished my game and went over to the seating area, I saw the tall and thin Governor going from table to table, chatting up people who came for the event or who were just there for a beer (I couldn't tell the random customers from the Hickenlooper supporters). Though this was a nice space in many ways, it was a very loud room and the row of pinball machines only added to the noise, particularly the classic Iron Maiden machine which "featured" the sound effect of a screaming woman. I hoped the campaign had a decent sound system in place.

John Hickenlooper was not one of the better known candidates, but I was aware of an intriguing bit of trivia about him because of work I'd done on Kurt Vonnegut. Vonnegut's last novel was the semi-autobiographical *Timequake*. In chapter 44, he wrote about a 1996 visit to Denver for a gallery opening featuring some of his prints. In honor of the event, a local microbrewery created a special beer, Kurt's Mile-High Malt. It was Wynkoop, the brewery co-founded by John Hickenlooper. It also turned out that Vonnegut had gone to college with John Hickenlooper's father, who had died when the future-governor was only seven. In the book, Vonnegut writes about regaling the future-Governor with stories about college days at Cornell, and he reprints a copy of the label of Kurt's Mile-High Malt.

I say all this because when Hickenlooper made his way around the room to me, we shook hands and I brought up his Kurt Vonnegut connection. Hickenlooper said that it was amazing to have had this coincidence come into his life almost at random. I joked that he and Vonnegut must have been in the same *karass*. That's a term from Vonnegut's *Cat's Cradle*, and it refers to a group of people who, unbeknownst to themselves, are spiritually linked or affiliated (sorry to be the literary geek here, but that's how it went down). Hickenlooper lit up at the reference. "I use that term all the time!" he exclaimed. Our connection made, I took a selfie and he continued working his way around the room.

Soon, I realized that Hickenlooper was going to individually speak to each of the 50 or so people in the room, taking the term "meet-and-greet" literally. It was not very interesting to watch a politician go from table to table, particularly when the room was too loud for the conversation to be heard. That said, I was pretty sure most of the discussions involved Iowans giving Hickenlooper unsolicited advice about how to run his campaign, the dispersal of such pearls of wisdom being the birthright of all Iowans. Anyway, there was still plenty of pinball to play. I made my way over to *The Shadow*, another 80s movie tie-in machine. Looking at the machine, I recognized that the backglass featured the likeness of Alec Baldwin from back in his movie star heartthrob days. That fact that Baldwin was now playing Donald Trump on *Saturday Night Live* seemed to connect up to my being here for a political event. Alec and I weren't quite in the same *karass*, but still, it was something.

Finally, even a pinball wizard such as myself had had enough, and I began to wonder when this event actually would begin. The governor had spoken to everyone he could, and I counted to see that seven people were trying to fix a microphone. Then, for no apparent reason, the microphone began to work and Hickenlooper began addressing the crowd.

I usually tried to shoot video of the first minute or so of a candidate's speech, but in this case I got footage of almost everything Hickenlooper said. Here you go:

"I see of all the different, different, uh...I guess you would say, different ecosystems and how different the West is from the East and the North from the South, that you cover so many different social ecosystems in one state, and yet the one defining thread—or, the two defining threads because they are connected—is that Iowa kindness, and everywhere I've gone people have been warm and receiving, and also everywhere I've gone I've seen people in Iowa looking out for each other, and that strength of community is, I think, what makes America special."

As far as sucking up to the local crowd went, this was not the best I had heard, and when I transcribed what Hickenlooper said, I saw that it was one of the longer, rambling sentences I hope to ever type. But he continued:

"I'm running for President—I'll give you the two minute pitch—I'm running for President because I feel like I'm the one person who has actually done what everyone else talks about. We are in the middle of a national crisis of division, and so much of what President Trump does—dividing us, pulling us apart—and yet in Colorado we've been able to engineer universal health care coverage in a bipartisan fashion, we became the number one economy in the country for the last three years (and for the last year I think we're going to be the number one rural economy), we beat the NRA with tough new guns laws, right, and we addressed climate change—we took on the oil and gas industry, and we got the first methane regulations (methane is 25% worse that CO_2)—"

Okay, I had quit recording there because apparently that sentence was too long for one take. But then about thirty seconds later, Hickenlooper finished his speech. He half-heartedly raised the possibility of taking questions from the audience before quickly dismissing the idea with a wave of his hand. Then he went back for another round of handshaking, even though he'd already met everyone in the room. Really, that was it? I felt like I hadn't quite earned my free beer. What was up with this? It felt like Hickenlooper just liked meeting new people and was using a presidential campaign as an excuse.

There were things we could have talked about. For example, I wanted to hear him say how he planned to win over Obama-Trump voters, since that was the general thrust of the case he was making. Also, during this event, a friend posted a reminder that Hickenlooper once drank a glass of fracking fluid to show how safe it was. Meanwhile, Colorado was experiencing an unprecedented number of fracking-related earthquakes. So, there were things we could have discussed.

I drifted over to the pinball machines but couldn't repeat my prior success on *Ghostbusters*. Then I regressed even further into my childhood, playing a round of Donkey Kong, Jr. Hickenlooper went behind the bar and got himself a beer. That seemed like a good idea. After taking on the Kong, I went up and ordered an IPA. When I looked up, the governor was gone, and the crowd that remained had either decided to stick around or hadn't been here for the meet-and-greet in the first place.

At the bar, a woman came up to order a couple drinks, using one of the Hickenlooper free drink tickets for an Old Style. I couldn't help but note to her that that seemed a poor choice at a brew pub with a decent range of selections (and, though I didn't say it, Old Style was really a poor choice at any time). The woman said it was for her husband, and she blamed his being a Cubs fan for his lame taste in beer. That didn't all make sense to me, but as she kept talking I realized she was even more confused than I was by all that had just happened. Her family had just been driving through from Illinois and stopped here for lunch. She wasn't fully sure who John Hickenlooper was. She didn't even realize they were attending a political event.

I took a sip of my beer. Well, I thought, I'm not sure this fully counted as a political event. But that seemed kind of rude to say, particularly from someone out of state who had just heard a really long sentence about how nice Iowans were. Instead, I said I hoped she had a good time on her visit. She left with her drinks. I gave *Ghostbusters* one last shot.

Chapter 13

Kamala Harris [6 June 2019]

Three events in one day! That's a lot to attend. Of course, many of the candidates had done the same thing, only they spoke at the events. I just had to show up and clap, so I was all in to see California Senator Kamala Harris speak at the Union Missionary Baptist Church in Waterloo. In fact, I had the whole family and some friends with me for this one.

Since I had started this project, my son, Nic, had started working as an intern for the Harris campaign. In fact, her campaign deserved a special shoutout for walking the talk and paying their interns. There were all kinds of reasons why this is a good development, and at the top of the list was the fact that Nic was now gainfully employed for the summer.

Of course, Nic's internship created a kind of weird situation in which I was going to write about an event and campaign that a member of my family was now involved in. So, let me state for the record that Nic's involvement with the Harris campaign will have no effect on what I write other than to give my son personal credit for everything that went right at the event. For example, though this Town Hall discussion was on a Sunday night, not a time when one would expect great attendance, over 200 people showed up, and the event was unique in that it started almost exactly on time. All of this was clearly due to my son. See, no conflict of interest.

The church's Fellowship Hall was packed with an upbeat crowd, one of the more diverse audiences I'd seen at a campaign event, and there was a great playlist streaming on the audio system. While it was accurate for me to say that the event started on time, which was true, there was a long wind up that made this possible, with a local speaker followed by five minutes of music, then another speaker and another five minutes of music. However, just when I began to despair that they were just stalling for time and the Senator was still in Cedar Rapids, she appeared on the stage.

Kamala Harris got a warm welcome from the attendees. She thanked everyone for coming out and introduced her husband, Doug Emhoff, who was in attendance. Harris was a polished speaker, and her stump speech was interesting in that she rarely addressed Trump directly, but she talked a lot about Trumpism, the beliefs and policies associated with the current administration. She was concerned with both Trumpism's causes and its impacts. This seemed a savvy way to advance her case without wasting her time persuading a crowd of people of something they already believed.

"This is an inflection moment in the history of our country. This is a moment in time that is requiring us each as individuals, and collectively, to look in the mirror and ask a question, that question being, 'who are we?' And I think what we all know is that part of the answer to that question is 'we are better than this.'"

The speech ranged from inspirational calls to policy details. In rolling out actions that a President Harris would take in her first 100 days (on gun policy and wage discrimination, in particular), she was able both to delve into specific issues and chart out a political path forward. She covered a lot of ground.

In the Q&A, I got to watch Nic run around in the crowd with a microphone. I took several pictures of him and only got his back. All of those pictures are too bad to share here. Harris's background as a lawyer and prosecutor clearly came to the forefront during this part of the event. When asked about marijuana legalization, she said she supported it in principle but had a series of caveats about the impact on young brains and questions about how to measure the impairment of drivers. When asked to sign on to the National Breast Cancer Coalition platform (Christine, again! Damn, she was everywhere!), Harris was able to speak about the work her mother did as a breast cancer researcher and how influential that had been on her as a girl. She was sure she would support the platform, but still, she wasn't going to sign anything without reading it. Once a lawyer, always a lawyer.

There was one memorable moment when a young man stood up to ask if he could make a statement rather than asking a question. "Oh, no!" I thought, a self-acknowledged grandstander is the worst at an event like this. I feared a long, indulgent rant. Maybe the Senator did too, but she said, "sure, it's a Town Hall" with an uncertain laugh. The young man then announced that he was a Republican and didn't agree with her on a lot of issues, but he appreciated her coming to Waterloo and hoped that as the campaign continued she wouldn't assume all Republicans supported the nasty tactics of late. That was it: very polite, very concise. Harris's response hit it out of the park, and it became the media moment from the event, so I'm going to reproduce much of it here.

"I want to thank you for being here. I want to thank you for having an open mind. Listen, part of the beauty of our democracy is that we debate, we discuss, we often will disagree but we have the same motivation. I know you're here because you love our country, and I'm here for the same reason, and we may have other different ideas about how we go about expressing that love and strengthening our country, but I know we're on the same page in terms of where we're coming from, and I know that about you because you're here right now and you had the courage to stand up and say what you said, and that means a lot to me. So, thank you. Thank you.

And on that point, I will say to you, that I truly, truly believe that some of the biggest challenges that face our country are not just bi-partisan, they're non-partisan. Truly, because look, even if November of 2016 had turned out different, we would still be—right now— a nation in flux, and a world in flux. Just think about it, around the world we have ascending and descending economies right now, right? Population shifts in large part because of climate change, right? We're in the midst of an industrial and digital revolution. There is so much happening—globalization. There is so much change happening in our country and in the world right now, and it then presents a question. It presents a question, which is a very significant one, which is what as a nation will be our standing? What will be our definition? What will be our strength? What will be our significance? I strongly believe these questions are at play in this election. It is so much bigger than, you know, the guy who's in the White House right now, which may be the motivation for a lot of Democrats. But I'm going to tell you guys, I believe there is so much more at stake right now. And the question will be are we going to hold on to our strength, but in a way that is respected and honored? Are we going to pay attention to the fact that, I believe, all of this disharmony, all of this staring at our belly button over the last couple of years, fighting each other, is making us weaker as a nation. It is making us weaker. The world is passing us by. I'm going to tell you, part of what I believe and I will say this now and I will say it again and again to anybody who will listen, including my colleagues who are across the aisle, as they say. We better come together and fix some of this stuff because ain't nobody else going to do it for us."

This moment of the speech went from empathy to a prosecutor-style building of an argument to a colloquial shout out to the audience. It was a real tour de force, and, from there, Harris finished with an uplifting conclusion to the Q&A, leaving everyone in a hopeful mood.

And, of course, then everyone wanted pictures. Plenty of people rushed the stage, phones in hand. Having learned lessons past, I was positioned between the candidate and the exit and got plenty of pictures: my daughter Devin and I with Senator Harris; my younger son, Ian, and I with Doug Emhoff; Nic and the other interns with the Senator. And then there was a sweet moment when Ian re-met Nora, Senator Harris's Iowa political director, whom Ian had worked with on the Hillary Clinton campaign as a 9-year-old volunteer. Of course, Ian was a foot and a half shorter the last time Nora had seen him. "Is that Ian?" she asked. That's how we'd all felt over this year of his growth spurt.

Later, I saw on the campaign's Instagram feed that even the guy who made the statement that I quoted above came up for a picture afterwards. All in all, this was a pretty successful event, marking the end of my long weekend of candidates. But, there were still more of them out there. This was the 13th event I had been to, and in July, Tom Steyer announced that he was running for President. At this point, even after seeing four candidates in a single weekend, I had begun to wonder if I would be able to get to at least 20 of them.

Chapter 14

Tulsi Gabbard [17 July 2019]

Hawaii US Representative Tulsi Gabbard was slated to participate in a "climate conversation" in Cedar Rapids on a day that had featured both scorching sun and torrential rain. Now, I know that weather is not the same thing as climate, but since this was to be an outdoor event, I wasn't sure what would be in store.

My experience in Iowa with Rep. Gabbard to date had been limited to seeing a "Tulsi 2020" billboard in the most oddly placed location I could imagine, on a state highway through Dyersville, a town of 4,000 best known as the site where *Field of Dreams* was filmed. Wait—I should be more precise. The billboard was actually on the outskirts of Dyersville where I was sure upwards of a dozen people regularly saw it.

And I was a little befuddled when the climate conversation was scheduled for 6 p.m., an odd time for an event, and one which likely meant I would have to drive and then catch a late dinner. So, I went in with a series of concerns, but all of them turned out to be unfounded.

The weather had turned more comfortable, and the event site was next to a Veterans Memorial Park in an area that I was familiar with, having been there for one of my daughter's track meets earlier this Spring. In fact, it was a unique location where a 360 degree view took in a stadium, an ice arena, grain silos, and a row of suburban-style houses.

However, best of all, it was a potluck! Here I was worried I was going to get hangry (not a typo, but that hungry/angry combination known to anyone who has parented a toddler), but the good folks of Cedar Rapids had set up a small pavilion area with a range of vegan-friendly salads, trays of fried chicken, and a big jug of lemonade. All was good. I dug in and settled down at a shaded picnic table.

By definition, outdoor events are more casual. People bring lawn chairs and pets, and it is understood that it is okay to chat up random strangers, particularly if you want to talk about the weather, which I was glad to do. The crowd was modest in size, I guessed around 50, and it seemed a group of usual suspects, Cedar Rapids area politicos and activists who seemed to know one another, as well as members of the local Veterans for Peace chapter. A number of the attendees had also gone to a candidate forum earlier in the day sponsored by AARP.

This event may or may not have started on time (having been properly fed, this seemed a less important issue to me), but once Rep. Gabbard's car made its way into the parking lot, things got underway quickly. A raised platform had been placed next to the pavilion, so that we were all able to keep munching away during the event. Gabbard was introduced by a local state senator, Rob Hogg, who had published a book on climate change and was holding a series of these climate conversations with candidates. Standing in front of an American flag rippling in the breeze, Gabbard began speaking about her concerns that climate change had become a divisive issue.

"The biggest frustration that I see in Washington is that once you bring up these two words—climate change—depending on the crowd that you're in, you'll either lose a whole bunch of people who are turned off because they see this as a polarizing issue, or you see others who then maybe look down on those who see climate change as something they don't want to talk about. Regardless, both sides are unfortunately, in many cases, drawing lines in the sand without actually breaking this down into what's real and what's important, how this impacts every single one of us. It comes down to protecting our environment."

Gabbard detailed how her upbringing in Hawaii (her sister was also in attendance) helped to make her an environmentalist. Hawaii's natural beauty was not a political issue. It was understood by all as something that needed to be protected and preserved. She was concerned that such stewardship was missing at the national level, that the U.S. had lost its role as a leader in environmental initiatives, particularly regarding climate change.

"Let's talk about how we can collectively take action to address this global crisis because that is what will be required. Yes, reentering the Paris Accords is an important first step, but even those who were signatories then knew and recognized that it wasn't nearly enough. It wasn't nearly enough to meet the kinds of targets and the kind of timeline that we need to see in order to stop this threat in its tracks."

Gabbard's main environmental initiative is the Off Fossil Fuels Act, a measure which, if enacted, would put the country on a path to 100% renewable energy by 2035 (at this point I was feeling pretty good about driving an electric car to the event!). It was one of the most ambitious resource-related bills introduced, though it had many hurdles to climb before becoming reality. But Gabbard said she was optimistic that change could be made across the partisan divide through slow, steady progress.

"Every single person here wants to make sure that our kids have a safe place to live and grow up in and prosper, that every American in this country will have clean water to drink, that we'll be able to wake up and have clear air to breathe. These are things that are central to all of our existence, and if we start our conversations there, we will find that agreement and that allows us to take another step forward, and then another step forward and then another step forward. And this is how we have to make progress to make the kinds of big change and big reforms we need to see here in the United States of America, so that we can be the kind of leader in the world that we should be."

Though Gabbard spoke in detail about her environmental policies, she spent at least as much time talking about her background as a combat veteran, and it was clear that that experience had shaped her view of government. Along with Pete Buttigeig (one of the other vets in the race) she lamented wasteful military spending, noting at one point that we spent $4 billion a month in Afghanistan but only $3 billion a year for major infrastructure needs.

I was particularly struck by that statistic and posted it out to my Facebook friends. The Facebook robots somehow interpreted that as my attempt to sell a "month" for $4 and turned my post into a classified ad. I wasn't so much offended by Facebook's misinterpretation of my post as by their lowballing the cost of a month at $4, only $3,999,999,996 off my asking price. The month remains available for purchase.

Back at the event, Gabbard was eager to discuss the losses of both people and money during the extended wars in Iraq and Afghanistan, even when her criticisms of the military-industrial complex led her astray from the topic at hand (though this also got one of the guys in the audience to shout out, "Thanks for talking about Dick Cheney's Halliburton!").

When we moved into the Q&A part of the event, my suspicions that this was a crowd of usual suspects was confirmed. Three people initially raised their hands with questions, and moderator Rob Hogg knew each of them by name. When asked, Gabbard made it clear that on day one of her administration she would end family separation on the southern border, a position that won her an eager round of applause. A question on the environmental impact of wars on native populations led her down a rabbit hole, however. Rather than discussing war and/or climate related migration, she extensively described the impact of toxic burn pits on soldiers. It's not that this issue isn't important, but it was only tangentially related to the question asked. Gabbard was very good when working on-script but didn't seem as adept on her toes.

But that off moment aside, she had a strong stump speech, showing herself to be knowledgeable and engaging. She also was willing to stick around for pictures. I worked my way through the crowd, patiently waiting in the picture line. When it was my turn to stand next to the candidate, I discovered that Tulsi Gabbard was surprisingly tall as she loomed over me while my picture was taken with her. All in all, this was a pretty well organized and efficient event. We were in and out in an hour, with dinner under our belts and plenty of time to enjoy a pleasant Iowa evening, climate change notwithstanding.

 Jim O'Loughlin posted an item for sale.
July 17 at 6:49 PM ·

month
$4

$4 billion a month in Afghanistan but only $3 billion a year for major infrastructure needs.

Chapter 15

Joe Sestak [18 August 2019]

So, here is the world we live in right now. When you saw the name "Joe Sestak," you likely said to yourself, "who?" Sestak is a retired three-star Admiral and a former two-term U.S. Representative from Pennsylvania. But, you are not alone in not knowing that. I had to look that information up on Wikipedia. Now, maybe some of this was Joe Sestak's fault. He entered the race late, and he had a history of pissing off party officials (more on that later), so perhaps he wasn't getting the benefit of the doubt. But Joe Sestak was running for President and was as qualified, if not more qualified, than many others in the race. That said, he had never cracked the top 20 threshold to make the debate stage, and he was unlikely to meet stricter requirements for future debates. Yet, still, he ran. The psychological and emotional motivations of any longshot candidate were likely pretty complex.

Joe Sestak was scheduled to appear at a meeting of our county's Democratic central committee. A warm, late-August Sunday night would seem about the worst time to get people together to see a candidate, so I wondered what the turnout would be like as Nic and I drove to the party headquarters. The party headquarters was just what you'd expect: a repurposed downtown building littered with candidate information and folding chairs. Campaign posters were randomly taped to the wall with the apparent purpose of sending Marie Kondo into a seizure. On a good day, someone brought cookies. If you were a risk taker, you could get a cup of coffee from an urn likely first used during the Carter administration. This was not a space where much thought was given to design. This was a place where people did work that had to be done, and it wasn't pretty.

This was also probably the only place where fifty dedicated politicos and activists (along with the organizers from every Presidential campaign with a local presence) could be found on a Sunday night in August. And there they were, usual suspects I had seen at many other events, the same people who can be counted on to come out to fundraisers, protests, and issue-related events. These were people you wanted on your side.

As a Presidential candidate, Joe Sestak got to jump the queue in the meeting agenda and address the crowd at the beginning of the meeting. I noticed that like several other candidates (Pete Buttigeig, Beto O'Rourke, Elizabeth Warren), he was rail thin, which apparently worked for you on television. He was casually dressed so as not to stand out in the come-as-you-are state.

And now is perhaps the time for a digression into the state of Iowa fashion. While I had heard the term come-as-you-are used before I had moved to Iowa, nowhere else have I seen it embraced so fully. Undoubtedly, this has roots in Iowa's rural tradition when the conventional long, hard hours of farming made dressing up a chore to be reserved for church on Sunday. And though far fewer people are directly working the land now, that tradition has persevered. I've seen people wear overalls to funerals and t-shirts with funny sayings to wakes. It's okay for students to come to class in pajama bottoms and nice restaurants are sweatpants-optional. With the exception of high school proms, I can't think of an event that is uniformly formal. Now, don't get me wrong, in many ways this is part of Iowa's unpretentious charm, and I like that clothing isn't necessarily a status symbol here. I'm a beneficiary of this when I realize, "no, I don't have to iron anything today." But there are some occasions that might seem to call for dressing as if you took your situation seriously, such as when running for President.

Anyway, when Sestak was introduced, he hopped right up and began pacing the front of the room delivering his stump speech. I often tried to post live video of part of a candidate's talk, and usually that was no big deal. But this time, I was sitting in the front row, and it seemed rude to stare at my phone when the candidate was standing directly in front of me. I tried to be polite and keep my eyes on Sestak rather than my screen, which resulted in some lesser quality footage.

Sestak began with a personal story, speaking of his daughter's battle with brain cancer. She had had a rare form of cancer with a low chance of survival, but she did survive. Sestak acknowledged that experience—both the quality of the medical care she received and the challenges the family faced in making sure she received it—as what motivated his entry into politics. He spoke about running and winning his House seat in a majority Republican district. While he supported a leadership-by-consensus model, opposing "a President who can only do executive orders," his policy proposals were more progressive than those from many candidates seeking some kind of middle ground. He also mentioned bucking the establishment to mount a primary challenge in 2010 to the Republican-turned-Democratic Senator Arlen Specter. Sestak described Spector as "the individual who had been permitted to try to humiliate Anita Hill." Sestak won that primary but lost in the general election to Republican Pat Toomey, who still holds that seat today. He didn't note that the loss of that Senate seat did not earn him friends within the Democratic establishment.

As Sestak spoke about the presidency, he reminded me a bit of John McCain—not in terms of his politics, but in the way that his Navy experience informed his theory of leadership.

"I'm in because I honestly believe there is a Hobson's choice. It's not just to elect a President but to elect someone people will trust because they believe he will always be accountable to them, even when they disagree well. To people, above party, above self, above any special interests, no matter the consequences. I believe if we do not unite this country, we can never meet the defining challenges of our time."

On day one of a Sestak presidency, he said he would close the gun show loophole, and he noted his past support of the assault weapons ban. He also supported a path to Medicare For All, but one that allowed for a slow process rather than a rapid transition. He only spoke for a few minutes (a kind of Presidential candidate elevator pitch), but he demonstrated an impressive grasp of details. And he sure needed to, because when he opened up the floor to questions, it was like a Presidential speed dating event. This audience knew issues and had likely seen more Presidential candidates than they could remember. They were not messing around. Gun control! Health care! Police brutality! Education! Answer fast! You've only got three minutes!

Sestak celebrated his experience in the Navy as a model for what could happen if we had different leadership in this country. His most animated anecdotes were drawn directly from his military experience, as when he discussed confronting racial intolerance within the ranks below him. And he would apply a similar sensibility to non-military situations. In response to the question about police brutality, he said he would handle it, "same as in the military."

"In the military you learn, 'expect what you inspect.' And the Justice Department should be into those types of...police districts and going through them if they are showing a propensity for that… But if incidents come up individually that are obviously discriminatory, they should be in there anyways doing those individual inspections."

The one disappointing thing was that, unlike Pete Buttigieg and Tulsi Gabbard, the other veterans in the race, Sestak never spoke about defense spending. That is unfortunate because veterans have a unique ability to raise questions about the military-industrial complex. At a time when the deficit was exploding due to the Trump tax cuts, 54% of all federal discretionary spending went to the military. Both Buttigieg and Gabbard were able to trumpet their military experience while arguing for reforms in defense spending, but Sestak didn't go there, and that was a missed opportunity.

Who knows? Maybe if he had had more time, that issue would have come up, but this was an atypical type of event and Sestak was just the opening speaker. Normally, I would have tried to get a picture with a candidate, but after he answered a few questions, there was still a meeting that had to happen. Sestak shouted out his email address and made his way out the door. The meeting came to order, and we got down to business.

Chapter 16

Michael Bennet
[1 September 2019]

 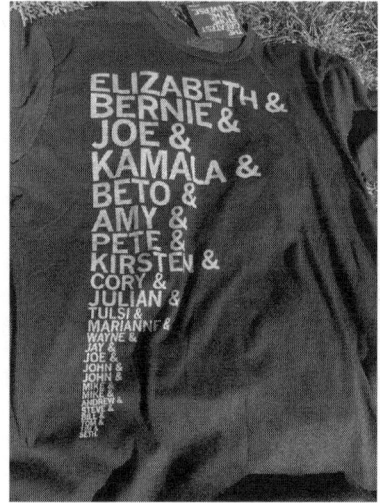

It was a beautiful late summer day in Iowa, and to get to an event in Cedar Rapids with Colorado Senator Michael Bennet I had to skip by all the food offerings at the NewBo City Market, ignore the art fair that had taken over the street, and bypass a busker who was playing Stevie Wonder-inspired harmonica. Missing the harmonica player hurt, but I was a man with a mission, even if my mission was arriving just in time for a town hall event with a presidential candidate.

This was the first event I had attended in a boutique, though Raygun was not a typical clothing store. Over the last decade it had become an iconic Iowa brand known for funny and snarky t-shirts that embraced all things Midwest (well, at least the good things: looking at you, Steve King). Still, it didn't seem like the kind of location suited to host a candidate. Would we have to move mannequins to sit down?

Once I got inside the store, I joined a cluster of people milling around the merchandise, and I discovered that Raygun was all in with the whole caucus process. The prime display spot in the store was dedicated to merchandise on the caucus and the candidates from t-shirts and pins to campaign biographies. And, in a touch that Raygun has become known for, some of the humor was hyperlocal. Take the t-shirt with the caption "Raygun: for the Iowa Caucuses, we're the progressive candidates' Pizza Ranch." If you live in Iowa, this is a very funny shirt. However, if you are an out of stater, this t-shirt probably makes as much sense as reading a 12-year-old's Snapchat feed. Huh? Pizza Ranch? What? But don't worry, I am here to help. I can dissect the joke to the point where it will both make sense and no longer be funny, but it will take me a few paragraphs.

1) So, Raygun was run on a shoestring out of Des Moines for a number of years, but from those humble origins, it has become a reliable indicator of midwestern millennial hipsterism and new urbanism developments. They now have a handful of stores scattered throughout the Midwest, including here as part of the post-2008-flood-revitalization of the New Bohemian section of Cedar Rapids.

2) Raygun has always worn its progressive politics on its sleeve (though this is perhaps a poor metaphor for an operation that is centered around short-sleeve t-shirts). Alongside slogans celebrating all things Iowa, like "Iowa: 75% vowels, 100% awesome," you can find t-shirts that say "America! The news is real. The tan is fake."

3) When you think of pizza, what's the first thing that comes to mind? Cowboys, right? No, well, then you can see part of the issue with Pizza Ranch. Now, I admittedly bring my bias into the following description as someone who grew up in an area with a large Italian population and plenty of good Italian food. The Pizza Ranch restaurant chain is based on the idea that people who don't really know what pizza is supposed to taste like will be satisfied with what they get served, which is doughy, cheesy

and with an oversugared sauce. Pizza Ranch was not designed to survive in a competitive marketplace with real pizzerias. Instead, it has carved out a niche in small, midwestern communities where regulars might not know to question pizza offerings like Texan Taco and Sagebrush.

4) But, the reason Pizza Ranch matters is that because the chain tends to be omnipresent in small towns (and has prominent Republican ownership), it often serves as a convenient location for GOP presidential candidates looking to hold meet-and-greets in conservative strongholds. Mike Huckabee credited his "Pizza Ranch strategy" with his victory in the 2008 Iowa Caucus. The Pizza Ranch circuit is a real thing in GOP circles.

5) So, when Raygun opened up its stores to many of the candidates from this cycle's Democratic race, they were essentially trying to reverse engineer the concept to create the Pizza Ranch circuit for progressives.

See, I told you I could explain the joke to the point where it would no longer be funny, and it only took me five paragraphs.

Anyway, back to the event. Finally, after milling around the store for a while, I realized that there was a second floor. I made my way upstairs and saw that the town hall was going to happen in a large back room that looked as if it doubled as a t-shirt storage and staging area. Chairs had been set up in front of t-shirt cubbies in a section where I imagine freshly snarky lettering would be drying on the front of shirts when there weren't any candidates in town. The senator would be speaking in front of a bunch of blue and white "Bennet for America" signs which reminded me of the gym uniform I had to wear back in the day when I attended Bennet Jr. High (no relation). When I posted this observation, it provoked friends to share a series of painful adolescent memories of polyester shorts and communal showers in locker rooms.

It didn't take long for Senator Bennet to arrive. He was dressed down for the occasion in jeans and an open collar shirt, and his introduction was no fuss as well. When Bennet began speaking he started off with a story about how his father has worked for the State Department, and Bennet was born in New Delhi. Normally, that anecdote only came up when the Senator was eating at Indian restaurants, but this was the week when the Trump administration announced it would no longer grant automatic citizenship to children of U.S. government personnel working abroad. By the time you are reading this, I'm sure a more recent outrage has supplanted that one.

Before being appointed as a U. S. Senator from Colorado, Bennet had been a school superintendent in Denver. Some of this came through in his speech, which went through a lot more American history than most.

"We lived in a Gilded Age once before, and I believe we're living in a Gilded Age now. The income inequality is greater today than it has been since 1928. We've got an education system —it pains me to say this as a former school superintendent—that is reinforcing our income inequality rather than liberating people from it because the best predictor of equality for education is your parents' income because that predicts where you'll live and that predicts the kind of school you'll going to go to. So, there isn't a chance to rise. For the last forty years or so, nine out of ten Americans essentially haven't gotten a pay raise."

He spoke of the role of compromise within the vision of the Founding Fathers, and he discussed the Progressive Era as a model for how to confront wealth inequality. He also returned frequently to his past as a superintendent when talking about issues ranging from health care to incarceration. "Our lack of investment in the future is unconscionable," he said at one point. I was listening carefully, but I was also occasionally distracted by the sound of the harmonica being played on the street right outside the store.

Bennet was one of the moderates running for the Democratic nomination. He had been vocal in his opposition to Medicare for

All, calling instead for a public option within Obamacare, which he argued would do more for underfunded rural hospitals that remain undercompensated by Medicare. That seemed a little too clever by half. It was unlikely that a Medicare for All system wouldn't revisit and improve the situation for rural hospitals, so this seemed a cheap shot to me.

There also were a few convoluted and even contradictory claims made by Bennet. On the one hand, he argued "you can't call yourself a progressive if you can't make progress," and he said an ability to reach across the aisle and compromise was essential. However, he also said that Mitch McConnell and the Tea Party cannot be compromised with; they have to be defeated at the ballot box. This raised a question. If you take Mitch McConnell and the Tea Party out of the Senate, who would be left to compromise with? Susan Collins? In fact, while Trump got his fair share of lumps in the speech, Bennet's most impassioned condemnations were directed toward Senate Majority Leader Mitch McConnell, whom he called out almost a dozen times.

In the Q&A, when asked by a woman in the audience about his policy on gun control, Bennet initially tried to discuss some of the challenges to immediate action, and his answer drifted into a call for increased mental health funding. This got him a dressing down from the questioner who reminded him that other countries have equivalent issues surrounding mental health but none have the problem with mass shootings that the U. S. does. "It's about the guns," the woman said passionately. Bennet did not disagree and he made a point of noting his support for universal background checks.

Toward the end, I was able to ask a question. I asked what a President Bennet would do on day one. I'd found it helpful to draw distinctions between the candidates (who agree on 80-85% of most issues) on the basis of what they thought had to be tackled first. This question helped to get to the candidate's priorities in the midst of the policy smorgasbord of a stump speech. Bennet replied that on day one he would reverse the Trump tax cuts, immediately tackle climate change, and then he cheated and listed about ten other things. No doubt it would be a busy first day.

In the end, though I didn't agree with Bennet on everything, he seemed knowledgeable and affable. It was nice to hear a candidate who placed educational issues toward the center of his vision, and I didn't have to wait in a long line afterward to get my picture taken with him. When the event was over, I drifted back downstairs and spent a little time browsing. I ended up buying a t-shirt that listed the first names of all the candidates who had thrown a hat in the ring for the Democratic nomination, and this was a shirt I felt I had earned, having seen 16 candidates to date.

Chapter 17

Joe Biden [20 September 2019]

When I saw that former Vice President Joe Biden was having a town hall event at a nature center in Cedar Rapids, I paused. I was all for nature centers, but they tended to be, well, in nature, and therefore not that close to many voters. So, I was not surprised when I drove down to Cedar Rapids and GPS led me far out of downtown into the outskirts of the city where I had never been before. It was a pretty ride along the Cedar River. I saw a cluster of wild turkeys and a gorgeously collapsed barn along the way. But, still, this place was far enough out of the city that I had trouble getting a reliable phone signal. Was this a good idea for a campaign event?

When I arrived at the Indian Creek Nature Center, cars were already sprawled out along the narrow country road in front of the center. It was a hot day, and chairs had been set up outside the center on an outdoor patio. The scene was pretty, but did I mention that it was hot? The Biden campaign handout doubled as fans for many in the audience, and people felt no shame in using umbrellas as parasols to ward off the sun.

Two other things stood out about the event. The crowd was notably old, which could have spoken to Biden's base of support or been due to the fact that this was a midday event, or required that you had to know the area pretty well to find this place. I estimated that over 200 people were there, a respectable if not exceptional turnout, but there must have been 100 media folks covering the event as well. I guess that was what happened when you were the national front runner.

Biden entered the race late and at the top of the polls. He had not been working Iowa as hard as some other candidates, and I had been unable to attend the one event he had had in Waterloo, next to where I live. Biden also had skipped a number of the cattle call-type events (though he was slated to participate in a sold-out LGBTQ forum later that day), so there hadn't been as many opportunities to see him, which accounted for his being down the list at number 17 of the candidates I'd seen.

Having initially put the wrong address into my phone (which led me to an isolated, gravel parking lot), I got to the event too late to get a chair, but that also meant I didn't have to wait too long for things to begin. The MC was state Rep. Rob Hoag whom I'd already seen at least twice before at other candidate events, and he explained why the event was being held here. It was the day of the Global Climate Strike, which I knew, but I hadn't made the connection with this location (duh!). The Indian Creek Nature Center structure met the "Living Building Challenge," which was so super-environmental I'm pretty sure it used sunshine to generate both power and happiness.

This was my first time seeing Joe Biden in person, though it is hard to remember a time when I didn't know who he was. He looked...like Joe Biden. In fact, with his mirrored sunglasses and open collared shirt, he seemed to be channelling the Joe Biden of the *Onion* or of *Hope Never Dies*. It was a good look. As with a number of other candidates I've seen, including Elizabeth Warren, Beto O'Rourke, and Joe Sestak, I was struck that someone who seems trim on television is actually rail thin in person. It was one of those weird TV things.

Of course, this date was also right at the beginning of the revelations of Ukraine-gate or whatever the scandal will eventually be termed, so that loomed larger in the moment, and I wondered if Joe Biden would address it during his remarks, but, no, he stayed right on message, focusing on environmental issues for almost all of his speech. Biden didn't mince words. Climate change was "the single most important issue" we were facing today, and it was hard to imagine anyone less well equipped to deal with it than Donald Trump.

"At a press conference after the G7, Trump was asked repeatedly about whether he believed in climate change. And all he could do was talk about America's wealth in fossil fuels. That was his response, 'We are so wealthy in fossil fuels.' Folks, all he thinks about is wealth for a very few people, that's all he talks about, for a very few."

Biden said of Trump that "everything he has done as President has made things worse." Biden listed rejoining the Paris Climate Accords as something he would do on Day One, and he pledged to convene a climate summit within the first one hundred days of a Biden administration. It was notable that Biden had a lot of details on his fingertips, including this bit that linked agricultural policy to environmental efforts.

"Farmers will be on the leading edge of the climate solution. American agriculture must be the first in the world to get to net zero emissions. There's incredible promise for carbon sequestration and storage in the soil. You know, I'm going to dramatically expand the conservation stewardship program."

Other shoutouts during the speech included electric cars and public charging stations. Biden was able to reference a lot of environmental legislation that he had previously supported, and he knew specific details about the Cedar River flood that had engulfed much of downtown Cedar

Rapids in 2008 (the river crested at over 31 feet, which was ten feet higher than the previous record).

He argued that making progress would require an ability to work across party lines. "You can't leave out entire sectors of society and expect that we're going to get things done. You gotta know how to negotiate. You gotta know how to bring people together, generate consensus… That's something I've spent my whole life doing. And I know everybody says 'well, you know you can't cooperate anymore.' Well, if we can't cooperate anymore, get ready—get your flippers out and, you know, your wetsuit—because we'd better be able to cooperate." It was a laugh line but one that provoked nervous laughter.

The stump speech part of the event wasn't too long, but Biden was happy to spend a lot of time answering questions. Note: that didn't mean that he answered a lot of questions, just that he spent a lot of time talking about those that were asked. Biden had a reputation for being somewhat long winded, and whenever an explanation evolved into a discussion of his early political career and the DelMarVa peninsula, I knew we were heading down a rabbit hole. But I will say that even when his responses seemed to go off in an unexpected direction, he did get back to answering the questions asked in the end.

At a certain point, people got distracted and began looking up into the sky. There was a bald eagle doing a flyover of the event, and someone interrupted to make sure the former Vice President noticed. That was a moment that no campaign could pay for. But at another point, the low point in the event, he was asked an environmental question and inexplicably veered into a defense of Obamacare. When he began going after Medicare For All proposals and defending private insurance plans, he got pushback from a woman in the audience (whom he brusquely dismissed as an Elizabeth Warren supporter). His critique of Medicare For All was later criticized as "bungled" in the *Washington Post*, which covered the event. Biden was much more effective when keeping his fire focused on Trump.

As things finally started to wrap up, I began to worry that people would start passing out from the heat. I made a halfhearted effort to join the scrum for selfies, but it was hard to make any progress in the crowd, and I'd never seen such media interest in the aftermath of the speech. Two different boom mics were in place to catch any stray bit of conversation that could be deemed newsworthy.

In the end, this event would likely have been considered a pleasant, if hot, oasis in Joe Biden's day. Though it began with news about Ukraine, he didn't have to talk about any of that here. Later the same day, he attended an LGBTQ forum and had a tense exchange with the moderator about his record and past statements. I have to think his afternoon at the Indian Creek Nature Center must have been the nicest part of this trip to Iowa.

Chapters 18, 19, 20
Marianne Williamson, Tom Steyer, John Delaney
[20 October 2019]

A threefer?! When I saw that there was an upcoming event slated to include three candidates I hadn't seen yet—Marianne Williamson, Tom Steyer and John Delaney— I knew that the time had come for me to attend my first cattle call.

"Cattle call" was the nickname given to events run by groups unaffiliated with campaigns but open to all candidates interested in attending. Some of these occurrences were huge gatherings, like the Iowa Steak Fry, which attracted over 10,000 people this year and must have literally involved a call to cattle, since it required serving enough steaks to prop up the Iowa beef industry for a year. Other cattle calls had been organized around specific issues, like climate change and LGBTQ issues, because during the Presidential caucus season if you build it, they will come. Well, at least some of them will.

It wasn't that I had actively avoided cattle calls up to this point, but I hadn't gone out of my way to attend any when I had the opportunity. I suspected these events would not be as quirky and interesting as many of the one-off gatherings put on by campaigns in locales hastily adapted for a town hall discussion. I mean, sitting in an echoey room at round tables and having people talk at me from a podium? I expected to be paid to go to something like that. But perhaps this one would be different. It was going to be held in Elkader (a small town even by Iowa standards) in a rural area not known as a political hub. And although a number of candidates would be there, none of them were in the top tier, so, okay, maybe this event would be unique. I was in.

The day of the event, I had to leave pretty early to get there on time, and it started to look like I had made a mistake. The hour-long route to Elkader was all on country roads, and it was a foggy morning where it felt like driving toward the edge of a cliff. But through careful steering and GPS, I arrived on time at a corrugated tin banquet hall behind a restaurant.

This was a "Passport to Victory" event that was part fundraiser and part designed to get big enough crowds into a rural location to make it worthwhile for the campaigns. It was a good idea, as it seemed to accomplish both goals. When I arrived and put down my money to get in, there were already about 200 people in attendance. For perspective, the population of Elkader is just over 1,200 people, so getting 200 people to show up is proportionately like having 1.4 million people go to a concert in Central Park (and even the giant 1997 Garth Brooks concert only attracted 980,000).

Okay, maybe that's trying too hard. It was still only 200 people, which was a respectable if modest turnout. And initially my fears were confirmed when I realized that sound was echoing throughout a room that was set up with a bunch of round tables scattered in front of a podium at the far end. But I did notice that there was a buffet table and a bar set up in the rear of the room. And there was a silent auction. On principle, I felt I had to put in a bid on one of the items, all of which had some local or handmade angle. I signed on for the Toppling Goliath six pack with an individually designed carrier. However, I worried that billionaire Tom Steyer would swoop in at the last minute and outbid me.

I made my way into the room and was glad to see a couple other usual suspects, party officials who had driven up from Black Hawk County and whom I regularly saw at such gatherings. I felt the relief of a middle schooler who had feared he would have to sit alone at lunch in the cafeteria. Soon we were joined by the chair of the state Democratic party, Troy Price. Flash forward: Price would go on to play a prominent role in the drama surrounding the caucus vote count and the malfunctioning app. In a work of fiction, I would have foreshadowed that by showing him having trouble with his phone or something. But, this is not a novel, and I can only report that Price was personable and friendly. He had driven in from Des Moines on what normally would have been a day off, and I had no doubt that he was one of the hardest working people in a room of hard working people.

As people continued filtering in, I opened up the program for the event and saw that, wow, 17 different candidates and elected officials were on tap to speak. The Presidential candidates had been sprinkled in throughout the itinerary as a way of ensuring people stuck around for the whole show. Apparently, anyone running for office from President to dog catcher had been invited. This was scheduled to be a four-hour event. Now, I realized that the buffet wasn't just a nice feature; it was necessary just to keep up endurance.

When things got underway, more or less on time, the first Presidential candidate to speak was Colorado Senator Michael Bennet. I had been to one of his events a few weeks earlier, and found him a smart and affable guy. But a more caustic version of Michael Bennet had shown up for the "Passport to Victory." He threw a few sharp elbows this time, taking swipes at Sanders's support for Medicare for All and Buttigieg's limited governmental experience. It wasn't the nicest speech, but he did have a pretty good dig when he noted that there were more students in the Denver Public Schools when Bennet had been superintendent than there were total people in Buttigieg's hometown of South Bend, Indiana.

One of the quirks of this event was that the room was arranged so that there was no backstage, which meant that candidates waiting to speak had to mill around in the crowd listening to the competition. It wasn't quite like being at Woodstock, but it was different to see Marianne Williamson chatting casually at a table in the back of the room while Michael Bennet stood in the front and made the case for a public option as part of an expanded Obamacare program. After Bennet had finished, there was a break in the action, and an announcement was made that the buffet was open. A line of hungry Iowans quickly formed, as did a queue of people looking to meet Marianne Williamson. In fact, I couldn't tell if they were the same line. But I was up for whichever way the line led me, so I took my spot in the rear. As the line snaked through the room, I went right by the table where Marianne Williamson was standing, got to take a picture with her, and then hopped right back in line to grab a plate of chicken, potatoes and green beans.

With lunch under my belt, I was ready for some serious listening, and best-selling author Marianne Williamson was ready to be listened to. Now, I will not be the first person to say this, but Marianne Williamson was not like other candidates. What most stood out was that her speech style had the cadences of slam poetry rather than congressional testimony.

"That conversation that too often Americans think of as politics is too narrow and superficial a conversation to contain the kind of energies that need to be released at this time. You see, ladies and gentlemen, within that conversation it's all about should be go left or should we go right. I'm telling you, it's not about whether we go left or right. It's about whether we go fresh or stale. You see, you need more than a passport. You need the right plane if you're going to get somewhere. And I feel very strongly about what that passport is. And the passport and the plane is not someone whose whole deal is that they're going to fight Donald Trump."

Okay, that's a lot to unpack: released energies, fresh vs. stale, passports and airplanes. In isolation a riff like this seems odd, but in the flow of Williamson's speech, I could see how it all fit within her bigger concerns. Her big target was anger and the corrosive effect such anger has had on politics and on American society at large. If politics was driven by anger (this was the plane), the candidate (this would be the person with the passport) wouldn't make much of a difference. We'd still be an angry country. So, the challenge she saw was to recognize why people were angry but then to find some other motivating force that could animate politics. In the end, her purpose was motivational, as one might expect from someone who made her name through appearances on Oprah (no disrespect to Oprah!). Williamson also was the first candidate I'd seen to end her stump speech with a call for Americans to "get all lit up."

The day went on. More local and statewide candidates spoke. There was a moving presentation about a local county chair who was fighting both cancer and her own health insurer. I may have gone for seconds in the buffet line.

Then Tom Steyer came into the room. He was a former hedge fund manager and current philanthropist who was a late entry into the race. He was a recognizable face from his many TV advertisements calling for action on climate change and then for the impeachment of Donald Trump. Because he was a billionaire and self-funding his campaign, I was pretty sure he could buy every building in Elkader without exceeding the limit on his credit card.

Again, because there was no backstage at this event, Steyer ended up hanging out in the rear of the hall when other candidates were speaking. During one of the breaks, I saw my moment and went up to chat with him. Somehow the conversation turned to our shared love of kayaking, and he talked about a yearly kayaking trip he goes on. I told him about the excellent river & lake kayak loop in Cedar Falls and Waterloo. Steyer was totally engaging and friendly, down to Earth without working too hard at it. After getting a picture with him, I picked his pocket and came away with a cool 3.5 million.

But Steyer had to wait for a while to take the stage. Hawaii Rep. Tulsi Gabbard, whom I saw speak over the summer, also spoke, though I only caught the end of her remarks. A surrogate for Bernie Sanders, California Rep. Ro Khanna gave a barnburner of a speech supporting Sanders and defending Medicare for All. I wouldn't be surprised if I saw him back in Iowa running his own Presidential campaign sometime in the future.

When Tom Steyer's turn came, he threw the crowd some red meat by saying that every Democratic candidate running against Trump was more qualified than "the criminal we currently have in the White House." Much applause followed. Counterintuitively, Steyer was trying to run as a kind of populist who was taking on corporate control of Washington. That wasn't usually the go-to position of a billionaire, but Steyer wanted to position himself as an outsider and as someone listening to voters.

"The thing that's the most important thing to me, and what I think has made me feel so strongly about what I'm doing is actually listening to people and actually hearing from you questions about what you care about but also your point of view. To me, I hope I can get through this and get some questions, because I'm very interested in a two-way conversation with people in this room."

Steyer had a pretty solid stump speech touching on a range of issues from gun violence to health care. It was a little tricky for a billionaire to make the case for giving power back to the people, but he handled the discontinuity with some self-deprecation. As some of my friends pointed out when I posted pictures, Steyer was also wearing a memorable multi-colored belt, and he had tweeted about it in the past. "Thanks for noticing my favorite belt! I bought it on a trip to Kenya from female artisans. I wear it as a reminder not to be so formal, and also as a symbol that the world is a better place when we educate women and girls."

By the time Steyer left the stage, he had plenty of energy to work the crowd, but I was getting pretty loopy. It had been over three hours and I had listened to at least a dozen speeches with more to come. As the last slate of speakers was announced, I noticed that Presidential candidate and former Maryland Rep. John Delaney was not mentioned. Since there was no place to hide in this venue, it looked like he was a no-show. Though disappointed, I had to admit that I was ready to hit the road, and leaving early wasn't going to bother me. I got in my car and started to drive off. Two out of three wasn't bad.

Suddenly, a huge bus came barreling toward me, racing like its tires were on fire. On the side of the bus I saw John Delaney's name plastered in large letters. It looked like he was going to make it after all. I turned off my GPS, pulled a U-turn and went back to the event.

Speeches continued. I made my way over to John Delaney, who was standing by himself in the back of the room and got a picture with him. He was polite if not particularly warm. It had likely been a long day for him as well. My first introduction to John Delaney had come when his campaign ran the first advertisement of the 2020 Presidential campaign during Super Bowl LII on February 4, 2018. I remembered when I saw the ad, my first response was, "who?" That was quickly followed by the realization that this was going to be a very long election season.

John Delaney served three terms as a U.S. Representative from Maryland after a successful business career. His early advertising in this race had made the case for bridging the divide between Democrats and Republicans, and he had positioned himself as a moderate running against the progressives in the party, sniping from the edge of the stage during a recent televised debate. I wondered if he might cut into other candidates today.

Delaney began by recognizing the recent passing of Elijah Cummings, his fellow House member and Marylander. However, that soon transitioned into a fairly generic stump speech about how everyone just needed to get along and how we needed a leader who could make that happen.

"And who is the leader that will do the most important thing that we probably need from our elected officials at this moment in time, which is to tell you the truth. Because I believe you deserve the truth, I believe you can handle the truth, and I believe for the last several decades you have not been getting the truth from so many people in Washington. Because the truth is if we want to grow our economy and grow it everywhere for everyone, we have to create the kind of environment where the private sector, the government sector and the nonprofit sector work well together."

I don't know. By this point I was kind of bored. Was I not being fair to Delaney just because he wasn't one of my top choices? Was I just tired and not giving him the same chance that I gave other candidates? That could be the case, but I noticed that the only moment when his speech got interrupted for applause was when he uncharacteristically called for some type of universal health insurance. That was more the temperature of the room, but Delaney didn't seem to read it well. Nevertheless, he deserved some credit for exceeding the speed limit to get here with enough time to give a short speech only to likely zoom back out in his bus-on-fire for another event later in the day.

Soon after Delaney finished speaking, the event began to wrap up. After more than four hours, I was pretty burned out, though a call for

Trump's impeachment still garnered several whoops from the crowd. Man, this group was committed! At the very end, they called out the door prize winners, and to my great surprise I heard my name! Not only did this mean that I was now the owner of a custom-designed and filled six-pack holder, but let the record show that Tom Steyer did not beat me in the silent auction.

Chapter 21

Andrew Yang [13 December 2019]

So, going into an event with California businessman, Andrew Yang, I knew that he was likely to be the last candidate I saw as part of this project. Of course, there was still a chance that "just call me Mike" Bloomberg would decide to cut out the middleman and start handing out $100 bills to Iowa voters, but I wasn't counting on that.

I finally got to see Andrew Yang when his campaign held an event at the Cedar Valley Unitarian Universalist Society, where I'm a member. Though the campaign was just renting the space (no endorsement implied), it was a location where I had heard plenty of sermons over the years, so I was ready for Yang to preach. It was an appropriately surreal final destination on my candidate tour, happening in the town where I live and in a familiar location that had been repurposed for a campaign. In fact, when I arrived, I immediately saw some familiar UUs who were either helping to stage the event or were in the audience.

It was also appropriate that I ended up sitting next to someone who was attending her first campaign event. As we sat around, waiting for Andrew Yang to arrive, we had plenty of time to chat. The person next to me was a mother with young children who had to get someone to watch the kids so that she could get away for an hour. When she asked me if I had been to many campaign events already, I had to hesitate. That fact that my kids were older and my job had more flexibility than most was what had allowed me to attend as many events as I had. Flexibility was even more of an issue when it came to attending the actual caucus, which required people to show up on a Monday night in February for at least two hours. So, yes, I had seen a number of them, I meekly told her.

"Is it normal that they start this late?" she very reasonably asked.

Wow, yes, was it ever.

However, all events must begin eventually, and so, too, did this one. This was officially a "Moms for Yang" gathering, so I was not surprised to see that Andrew Yang was here with his wife, Evelyn Yu, and that she was introduced first. Yu had formerly worked in marketing, and she was notably "on brand" while delivering more than just a "my husband is a nice guy" speech. She mentioned Yang's signature policy, the "freedom dividend," which was a form of universal basic income that would ensure Americans each received a monthly $1000 payment to do with what they saw fit. Often, Yang's "freedom dividend" was promoted as both a safety net and as a prime-the-pump kind of incentive that would increase economic activity. However, Yu celebrated it as a formal recognition for the work of unpaid caregivers, such as mothers.

When Andrew Yang joined his wife at the front of the room, he made a point of acknowledging her efforts as the primary caregiver for their children, including a son with autism, whose special needs required a great detail of attention and patience. He spoke in very personal terms about how unprepared they had felt for the demands of responsibility that were thrust upon them by parenthood.

Yang was difficult to pigeonhole. He was a businessman who had not previously held elective office, but he was not running as an anti-government candidate, unlike some other businessmen-turned-politicians who will remain unmentioned. In fact, Yang supported progressive programs like paid family leave, though he did so by arguing that this big public expenditure would be good for business in the end. His hard-to-categorize quality also came out when he was discussing health care. He was a supporter of Medicare for All, the single-payer alternative/ expansion to Obamacare. However, he favored a slower rollout than Bernie Sanders and Elizabeth Warren, and he argued that because M4A would be cheaper and more portable than existing employer-based plans, no one would need to be compelled to join.

"We need to put coverage in place and then sweep the private insurers out of the market over time, but you don't legislate that. What you do is you demonstrate it through saying, look, this is actually more efficient, more affordable, lower stress and higher quality. I'm confident we can do that because, just like you, I've looked at the inside of the health care system, and I've seen just how much money is getting spent on things that have nothing to do with our health."

He made it all sound pretty easy, and he drew on his experience in business to illustrate how this "wither on the vine" approach to our current health insurance system would work.

"As someone who's run a company, I spent a lot of time on health insurance, even though health insurance had nothing to do with my business. You know, it's like, you have plans, you go to employees, you say, 'hey, here are the premiums, here's what you pay for, you pay for this.' A couple things: number one, prices only ever went up. Like, the health insurance company never contacted my business and was like 'Great news, it's going down this year.' It never happened in American history.

Number two, if someone had come to me, let's call it the government, and said, 'hey, guess what, there's this new public option, and you can get insurance off the back of your business, and you pay into the system,' I would have jumped for joy. Because it wasn't just the money, it was the fact that I had to become an expert in health insurance even though it had nothing to do with my business. I had to have difficult conversations with my employees about their health insurance, which also, I wanted to be none of my business. And, so, even if the economics were exactly the same, I would have been thrilled with some sort of public option. So, if we provide the public option and provide employers that kind of choice, then the employers are going to do our work for us because employers are going to look up and say, 'Hey, guess what, there's this public plan, it's going to be great for you,' and that's how we convince the American people over time."

One thing that stood out was that Andrew Yang was having a great time. He was comfortable in front of a crowd and seemed to enjoy the attention from a group of well wishers who would laugh at his jokes. My favorite was when he noted that each Iowan was worth 10 Californians, politically speaking. He didn't speak for long, but when he opened up to the crowd for questions, things got really interesting. It must have been because both he and his wife spoke about the challenges of raising a special needs child in very personal ways. Or maybe it was just the type of people who were drawn to Yang's candidacy. Either way, people soon began volunteering heartbreaking stories of struggling with mental illness, whether their own or that of a family member. Accounts of the turmoil, both personal and financial, diseases like schizophrenia could bring about quickly came to dominate the discussion.

Yang's response was surprising to me. On the one hand, he was an emotionally intelligent guy, and he ended up giving a lot of hugs to people who spoke while clearly feeling for their situations. But, on the other hand, he was more than willing to go off script and riff about something he read regarding the hit-or-miss nature of anti-schizophrenia drugs. While his wife, Evelyn, made sure to stay on message, it didn't take much to get Yang to meander way off topic. However, eventually he would reel himself back in, stating, for example, that one of the good things about the freedom dividend was that it was not income dependent, which made a difference for any family that was only one tragedy away from having everything come undone.

The quirkiest moment of the day was when a veteran in the audience chimed in to argue that when he returned home after a deployment and struggled, it was easy to be prescribed antipsychotic drugs that didn't help him. However, on his own, what he found did work was psilocybin mushrooms, and he argued it was wrong that such drugs were considered beyond the pale for use by the VA. Yang was up for this discussion. His policy on marijuana is basically libertarian/legalization, and he was happy to come out as pro-'shrooms as well. Somehow this answer eventually devolved into a thought experiment about what would happen if the VA did a study involving shamans prescribing mushrooms. Where were we again?

Anyway, the wonkish moments in the event were also notable. Yang had a lot of specific, outside-of-the-box policies he supported and had detailed in his speeches. Though the U.S. had never had a value added tax, which was common in Europe, he supported a VAT as a way of capturing revenue which was otherwise too easy for large companies like Amazon (which paid no U.S. federal income taxes in 2018) to avoid.

Yang was also down on robots. Well, specifically, he was worried that advances in artificial intelligence were likely to eliminate large categories of work in the future. While, historically, it has been a sucker's bet to say that new technology will eliminate jobs altogether, there's no doubt that technological disruptions can have huge impacts on individuals and if, for example, self-driving vehicles led to the elimination of truck driving as an occupation, that would wipe out the single largest category of male employment in the country. Already retail sales jobs, the single largest category of female employment in the country, had suffered under the onslaught of e-retailers like Amazon. Yang noted that he hasn't spoken to anyone involved in AI research who was not concerned about future implications, and, for Yang, this was yet another reason why a universal basic income program was needed.

Though the woman sitting right next to me needed to dash out before the speech was over to get back and relieve her babysitter, I was able to stick around and get one more candidate picture. It was likely my last one of this cycle—I had seen 21 candidates over almost twelve months and gotten selfies with the majority of them— so you might have thought I'd have a more natural smile by this point, but no. It was a good thing I was not the one running for office.

Part Two

The Caucus

Chapter 22

Memories of Caucuses Past I [Introduction & 2000]

Rather than jump right into my experience of the 2020 caucus, I want to detail my prior experiences with caucuses in Iowa, both to give some background and explain how the process functions. Admittedly, this approach allows me to use the tried and true technique of delaying the conclusion of their narrative by introducing a vital flashback just when it seems like things are about to come to the end. So, buckle up, we are going into the wayback machine.

Of course, since I had not planned to write a book on this topic, I'm forced to rely on my recollections, and I wish I was one of those people with a steel trap memory, but I'm not. To illustrate, I recently saw on social media that a high school friend had posted, under "Albums I Love," the cover of a Police record. I remembered that he and I had seen the band on their concert tour for that album, and I posted that, feeling pretty proud that I had recalled that detail. My friend responded with a joke about that being the night someone's hair was set on fire. Umm.... that doesn't seem like the kind of detail one should forget, but, I'm afraid to say, I had nothing. So, I'll do my best in what follows.

When Julie and I (with then-two-year-old Nicky) moved to Iowa in the Fall of 2000, we were too late for that year's caucus, which had been an open field for both the Republicans and Democrats. On both sides, the caucus victors (George W. Bush and Al Gore) went on to win their party's nomination, and Iowans took pride in their ability to prognosticate. I showed up too late for the party, and I only had a vague sense of what the caucus was about at that time. It only became more baffling to me when I heard people talk about how they had temporarily changed their party registration to go to whichever caucus seemed to have had the more interesting race. Really, I thought? People talk about switching party registration as if they were going to check out the new restaurant in town. And what did it mean when people talked about things like viability and re-alignment? I would soon find out.

Chapter 23

Memories of Caucuses Past II [2004]

In 2004, Julie and I attended our first caucus. This was the year in which John Kerry was a come-from-behind winner in a race that also featured Howard Dean, Dennis Kucinich, Dick Gephardt and John Edwards. By then, little Nicky was six-year-old Nicholas, and Devin was all of two. There must have been a process involved with getting a babysitter for the night, as there would have been for all of our other friends with small children, but I don't recall it being a problem. The caucus was held at our local Lincoln Elementary School, which was then an old, three-story building with narrow hallways.

We arrived at the caucus with the mistaken impression that we were about to do something similar to voting. We were in for a rude awakening. At the sign in, I saw that a number of the elected city council people on the non-partisan board were working the table. I hadn't thought a couple of them were Democrats, and this was the first of several surprises. At the sign in, we were also asked to announce our initial candidate preference, a question which no poll worker would ever ask, but this was so we could be sent in the right direction. Candidate clusters were split off into different classrooms rather than all gathering in one room (which seems really weird the more I think about it). It seems a decision was made to group candidates by where on the political spectrum they stood, so that the Edwards and Gephardt groups were off in a completely different room. Then we stood and stared at which of our neighbors were supporting which candidates. This was shocking to me at the time, and it seemed kind of voyeuristic. It still does.

In the lead-up to the caucus, there had been a lot of discussion of candidates and strategies among our friends. On the progressive side, the ongoing wars in Iraq and Afghanistan were the animating issues, and people were split between Howard Dean and Dennis Kucinich. I had been persuaded by the argument that in the caucus you should go for the candidate you most agreed with rather than trying to play some guessing game about electability. So, though Kucinich was a longshot candidate by any measure, that's who Julie and I agreed on independently.

Still, we were surprised when we saw that a friend and colleague, John, was the main Kucinich organizer for our precinct. This was the first we had known that he was a Kucinich supporter, though maybe that shouldn't have been surprising since we had attended a number of protests together during the George W. Bush administration (pick your issue). He was at the center of our group, wearing a Kucinich t-shirt and with clipboard in hand. We were ready to be guided toward whatever was to happen next.

We counted off and then we stood around. Every once in a while someone else with a clipboard came over and asked how many people we had. The main concern was that no one go anywhere before the count was official (which was exactly what you would do if you were voting instead of caucusing). This was where I first became acquainted with how the delegate process worked.

Lesson one of Caucus School was that caucusing was not at all like voting. Though the system was tweaked over the years, the process that the Democrats used was particularly arcane. While we were counting how many individuals supported a candidate, in the end, that number did not matter. What mattered was how many county convention delegates each candidate would receive. So, for example, if there were 250 people in our precinct and the lords on high had decided that our precinct had 10 delegates, then each 25 supporters a candidate had would count for one delegate. Of course the math never worked out so elegantly. Over the years I seemed to recall a lot of dividing by seven and trying to decide whether to then round up or round down.

But that wasn't the confusing part. I haven't even discussed viability yet. When you came into the caucus and stated your initial preference for a candidate, that was not binding. The reason for this was that once the initial count was taken, any candidate that did not have at least 15% of the total number of people at the caucus site was declared "non-viable," and that candidate's supporters could join another candidate's group, declare themselves "uncommitted," go home, or (so the rumors went) be wooed by an offer of homemade baked goods. Up until 2020, you could change your mind after the initial count even if your candidate was viable. During the chaotic period of "realignment" if you dared to go to the bathroom you would be suspected of trying to switch camps. Then, once realignment had happened, there was another count, and on the basis of that calculation, a number of delegates would be assigned, and each campaign then had to scrounge up volunteers to be county convention delegates.

And, then, for some reason that never made sense to me, once it seemed like the caucus was over and everyone was ready to go home, the people in charge would begin insisting that we were, in fact, at a meeting and that it was now time to make convention platform plank proposals.

At some point, exhaustion would win out and people would be allowed to go home, but the process took hours.

In 2004, I didn't really understand all of that, but I assumed that John did, so I paid attention to what he asked of us. When the initial count was done, he was pretty excited to see that it looked like Kucinich was viable. John had been involved with past progressive campaigns (Jackson, Nader), and, though he was in for the long haul, he didn't expect anything other than an uphill slog. Even after realignment, when Gephardt surprisingly was non-viable, the Kucinich campaign still had enough support for one delegate. We were all pretty happy with that. If our precinct was any kind of indicator, maybe an unexpectedly strong showing by an anti-war candidate like Kucinich could change the public conversation. When all was over (and it wasn't fast), we went home and waited for the results.

That was when I realized that our precinct was not a bellwether. Though I had never considered where I live a particularly progressive area, we were a university community and a population center within Iowa. The one delegate Kucinich got in our precinct was one of only 39 he got statewide, for an unimpressive 1.3%. The story of the night was John Kerry, who came from behind to win with 37.6% of the delegates. Well, actually the story of the night was that Howard Dean, who had seemed to be surging as an anti-war candidate, ended up performing less well than expected with only 18%. That night his concession speech aimed to keep his supporters fired up, and it ended with a whoop that became known as the "Dean scream." His campaign never got back on track. 2004 was a year when Iowa did pick the eventual nominee, though John Kerry (with John Edwards as his vice presidential nominee) would go on to lose in the general election. For me, it was a surreal introduction to the Iowa caucus.

Chapter 24

Memories of Caucuses Past III [2008]

That brings us to 2008 and the event that has become one of our favorite family stories. It may be hard to remember, but when Barack Obama began his Presidential campaign, he was considered something of a longshot. As a first-term Senator who had opposed the war in Iraq, in a country that had never elected a non-white President, there was no sense of inevitability around his candidacy. In fact, he was more curiosity than celebrity when he declared his intention to run for President. The first time Obama came to Cedar Falls, in the summer of 2007, he spoke in a downtown park in an open bandshell. That day, our then nine-year-old son, Nic, had a dentist appointment within walking distance of the park. It was a nice day, so Julie took him to his first political event. There were maybe 100 people there enjoying the nice weather.

Obama had brought his whole family, and after introducing them, he said that Malia and Sasha (who must have been around nine and six at the time) had seen their dad give plenty of speeches before, and they were going to go across the park to the local historical society where there was an exhibit on dolls. And then Obama spoke. As you now know, the man can give a speech, but he was still a fairly unknown quantity. Julie was impressed, as was nine-year-old Nic.

At the end of the speech, it was announced that people could line up if they'd like to shake hands with Obama (this is what was done in the era before phone selfies became common). Nic asked if he could get in line. Julie looked at her watch (see, smartphones still weren't quite a thing).

"No, you have a dentist appointment," she said. "You can't be late."

"But, Mom," Nic said, with the earnestness that one would expect from a nine-year-old whose first political experience was seeing Barack Obama speak in his hometown park. "He could be the President of the United States, and I could shake his hand."

"Oh, honey," Julie replied, lowering her voice slightly. "He doesn't really have a chance of being President."

And so they went to the dentist.

Needless to say, Nic has never forgiven his mother. In fact, the story comes up every once in a while when we want Nic to take out the garbage or when we cut off his complaints by noting all that has been done for him.

"Yeah, but I could have met Barack Obama, and you made me go to the dentist."

There's not much to say to that.

By the next time Obama came to town, his campaign was in full swing. He spoke to packed gymnasiums, and there would not be another chance for Nic to shake his hand.

As the 2008 caucus approached, both Julie and I had become Obama supporters. By this time, Ian had been born and we had three children, aged nine, six and almost two, so we knew ahead of time that getting to the caucus was only going to be slightly less complex than launching the space shuttle. We had to plan in advance. Because we both taught college classes, we had an available supply of babysitters, but we didn't want to ask someone to babysit who might also want to caucus. That would just cancel things out. We wondered which students of ours might not be Obama supporters. This is not the kind of question one asks a student, so we had to guess. We asked a student we liked very much but who seemed apolitical. She said yes. As a bonus, she also agreed to stop by the house and feed our cats over Winter Break when we would be visiting our families back east. Things were falling into place, and we were all in. Before we left for the holidays, Julie got a call from one the local Obama organizers. He asked if we could help house any volunteer canvassers coming in from out of state. They'd hardly be in the house at all, we were told. They just needed a place to crash.

The timing was perfect. Our house was available, and we just let them know to expect someone dropping in a couple times a day to feed the cats. We arranged to leave keys, one for the campaign and one for our cat feeder/babysitter, and left for the holidays feeling like we had done our part.

A couple days later Julie got a call on our cell phone–yes, we shared a cell phone, and it was a pay-by-the-minute flip phone; people used to live like that. It was one of the Obama organizers. We weren't even sure how he had gotten our cell number. There was a sense of urgency in his voice.

"Julie, you have to release your babysitter!"

"What?" Julie replied, not sure where this conversation was going.

"You have to release your babysitter. I was talking to her when she came in to feed the cats, and both she and her boyfriend would caucus for Obama, but she can't if she's babysitting for you that night, and if she doesn't caucus her boyfriend won't either."

"But we need a babysitter that night. We have three small kids."

"The campaign is going to have on-site childcare at your caucus site. You can bring your children with you. These are two people who won't otherwise caucus. They're not even on our lists. When you look at the costs of the campaign, it's about $250 for each person that turns out. This would be like making a $500 donation."

There was hesitation. We had a plan in place. Things were set. But, of course, we were persuaded to "release our babysitter." We would bring our kids to the caucus with us. That would be fine, wouldn't it?

Caucus time arrived on a cold January night (I haven't actually checked on the weather, but it was January in Iowa, so I'm pretty confident with my guess). Dinner must have been quick and unexciting. I'm guessing macaroni & cheese was on the menu. To get to the kids' school where the caucus was again, we had to bundle up the three of them in their winter gear. We lived four blocks from the school, but it could be a cold, if familiar, walk at night.

By this time, the old Lincoln Elementary School had been replaced by a shiny new building with spacious hallways and a much larger cafeteria. This was a good thing because our precinct was crammed into the cafeteria and the turnout was huge (in fact, almost double what it had been in 2004). Though the cafeteria had tables that must have seated almost 200 people, those seats were long gone when we arrived, children in tow. We found someone from the Obama campaign who told us that the babysitting was in the kitchen area adjacent to the cafeteria. This gave us pause, and for good reason. The distinguishing feature of the kitchen was the toddler-head-high metal rail for trays that ran the length of the buffet line. But, not to worry, the kids weren't going to be restricted to that area. They had the run of the entire kitchen and could play among the food preparation equipment.

Okay, now you can start worrying because by the time we got there, there were about a dozen kids, of varying ages and temperaments, and a lone babysitter, a teenage girl who was too young to caucus, and who had the deer-in-the-headlights look of someone way in over her head.

Things were already spinning out of control. Some kids were chasing each other, and others were whining for their parents. The only thing none of the kids were doing was sitting at the small coloring table that had been brought in, which held a box of crayons and a few pathetic, photocopied pages. Yeah, I couldn't blame the kids. It also became clear that though the Obama campaign had arranged for the babysitting and kept track of how many kids would be there, random Clinton supporters, festooned in Hillary stickers, were dropping off their kids as well, only adding to the chaos.

It was here that I made what will go down in history (make that, History) as my greatest political contribution. Heading into the night a little worried about how things might go, I decided at the last minute to bring along our portable DVD player. Back in 2008, this was still noteworthy technology, and we had gotten a lot of mileage out of it (literally) to keep the kids happy during long car rides back and forth to visit our families.

When I witnessed the chaos in the kitchen, I leapt into action, taking out the DVD player and setting it up on a shelf that was at kid viewing height. We only had the one DVD that was already in the machine, from the series *A Pup Named Scooby Doo*, one of the many spin offs that we came to know all-too-well at that time in our lives. I turned it on and a calm settled over the room. Kids stopped running and came over once the DVD began to spin. In retrospect, I realize that the DVD player screen was only slightly larger than that of some current smartphones. But, in 2008, in a kitchen with no other non-hazardous activities, this was enough. Children of all ages huddled around the player like ancient human tribes once stared into bonfires—well, if bonfires had had animated puppies.

Disaster averted, Julie and I went into the cafeteria. Because 2008 was an election year without an incumbent and at the end of George

W. Bush's unpopular second term, it attracted a pretty broad field, and as I scanned the room, I could see friends and neighbors supporting Joe Biden, Hillary Clinton, John Edwards, Dennis Kucinich, Barack Obama, and Bill Richardson. The model remained the same. We closely clustered with other Obama supporters, as the lead organizer tried to keep people from drifting away, and we tried different methods of counting a large group of people. The winner: a gym-class style technique where everyone holds up a hand and only takes it down once one has been counted.

I was taken aback by how many of those standing with me I had never seen before. We all lived in the same neighborhood, but most of these people were strangers to me. As the counting was going on for the initial alignment, Obama had the biggest group, and Clinton and Edwards were also viable. The Richardson group was close, but they did not appear to have the numbers to make the 15% threshold.

Well, by now, with one other caucus under my belt, I was an old pro at this and understood how the game was played. I waltzed over to the Richardson group hoping to persuade a couple of friends to come over to the Obama side. However, the Richardsonians were not to be deterred. They were chanting and trying to lure enough people into their camp to become viable. When I got close they started shouting and gesturing to me to come over and join them. I beat a quick retreat back to the safety of the Obama camp, and I relieved Julie of little Ian, whom she had retrieved for a break from the Kitchen of Chaos.

A cheer went up from the Richardson group, who apparently had corralled a couple stray Biden supporters and had reached the threshold. We went into the second round of counting, and I struggled to hold a toddler while keeping one hand in the air. It was a big night for Obama in our cafeteria. He easily defeated Clinton while Edwards and Richardson were also rans. When the counting was complete, we skipped the rest of the event, gathered up our kids and DVD player and headed for home.

We put the kids to bed and settled down for what I expected, after the Kucinich experience of 2004, would be another disappointing set of results, as our precinct would likely once again be an outlier within the state of Iowa.

Of course, that wasn't what happened at all. It turned out to be the night the Obama campaign took off. His victory in Iowa and a stirring victory speech was the spark that lit up the campaign. Though it wasn't a straightforward path to the nomination, the Iowa caucus came to be seen as a seminal moment in the race. Obama won big and he won throughout the state, in both urban and rural counties, while Clinton and Edwards were neck-in-neck for second. Clinton wound up with more pledged national delegates but Edwards had more State Delegate Equivalents (and, no, I'm not going to try to explain the difference) The main takeaway was that it was a big night for Obama. Even with my poor long-term memory, I still remember that.

Chapter 25

Memories of Caucuses Past IV [2016]

In between 2008 and the next contested caucus in 2016, a lot had changed. For our family, the main thing was that our kids had grown a lot. In particular, Nic had gone from needing a babysitter to interning for the Hilary Clinton campaign. He spent countless hours door knocking and phone banking, and he even persuaded his little brother Ian to join him for phone banking. Ian became a campaign mascot known for wolfing down snacks at the headquarters and for his unique pronunciation of the name "Debra," which a nine-year-old reasonably thought rhymed with "zebra."

So, with all that good karma, of course, we were a united family for this one, right? Well, no, this year we were a family divided. I had been a longtime Bernie supporter and Julie was also with Sanders. Devin decided that since she was too young to vote, she was going to stay out of the fray and remained uncommitted through it all. Our front lawn had dueling yard signs, but for the most part we were able to stay civil despite supporting different candidates.

By the time caucus night rolled around, Nic had become a precinct captain, and he had to eat an early dinner and get down to the school early. Julie and I made sure everyone was fed, glad that Devin was old enough to watch Ian so that we didn't need to go through any babysitter drama. However, by the time we got kids fed and dishes washed and made it to the elementary school, we had arrived just before the doors were closed and they stopped letting people in. I know this because I have a picture of the woman directly behind us in line who was forced to carry a sheet of paper that said "Last person" on it, as if she was the Final Girl in a horror film. We brought up the rear of the long line to sign in, and we waited.

However, there was one notable change in this year's caucus: I had gotten a smartphone and now I was able to take pictures and post information about my caucus experience in real time to friends via social media. I was struck at the time that this was popular with the peeps, particularly those who were in far-flung states awaiting results from the caucus, this unusual and arcane thing from Iowa (not unlike detasseling in that regard). When we finally registered and got inside the cafeteria, people were all just standing around and we got to say hello to Nic. But we had to be quick about it. He was on the clock and had plenty to do.

An announcement was made that there were 372 people in our precinct (watch this number!), and, after crowdsourcing the math, that meant that candidates needed 56 supporters to be viable. And, then the games began. There was another announcement telling us that it was time to be counted in our preference groups, and like a science experiment involving the formation of cells, we began the great shuffle, awkwardly clustering into different parts of the cafeteria, all the while looking around the room to see who our neighbors were supporting.

Once we were all packed together close enough to fit in a sardine can, we raised our hands and counted off. This took longer than it would have taken a similar sized group of Kindergarteners using the same cafeteria, but eventually we did get the initial count: Bernie 250, Hillary 100, O'Malley 11, undecided 9. If you are good at math, you will notice that that only comes to 370. What happened to the other two people in the initial count of 372? Did they go home? Were they kidnapped? Murdered? Eaten? It was a mystery.

Then it was time for realignment. We were temporarily allowed to roam around a little bit. Julie and I saw Nic trying to recruit an O'Malley supporter, so we gave him his space. When we came back for the second count it was: Bernie 255, Hillary 107 undecided 6, O'Malley 5. Again, for the math whizzes reading this, that added up to 373. Hurrah! The missing couple had not been eaten! Apparently, they were just busy giving birth to another registered voter. And, also, what was with the O'Malley people? Once it was clear he wasn't going to make the viability threshold, what was the point of sticking with him? That made less sense than hanging around for two hours to declare yourself "Undecided."

Now it took more math to figure out delegates. Bernie got seven and Hillary got three. But remember, we were far from done. People had to volunteer to be delegates. Across the room, I saw Nic instructing the Hilary supporters in the arcane details of this process. Later, a friend in the Clinton group wrote, "Nic did a great job, even if it took me a bit of time to realize that was little Nicky telling us what to do. So cool!"

Then there were platform proposals and even a pass the hat fundraiser. Would this night never end? After things started winding down, we got to check in with Nic. I wondered if he would have been disappointed that Clinton hadn't done better in our precinct. But, no, he was in great spirits and had had a wonderful night in his element. We stuck around and helped clean up the cafeteria. Unless you were a stickler for math, this caucus seemed to have been pretty well managed.

We all walked back to the house, but Nic was then off the campaign headquarters to watch the results. He may have lost the battle, but he won the war. It was a close contest and not without some controversy. There were disputes over delegate counts and when tie votes necessitated the need for coin flips to award delegates, the coins were clearly on Clinton's side. According to media sources, Clinton won six of six (or maybe seven) coin tosses. Even after an extensive Snopes.com investigation, it was still difficult to determine how many loose-change-awarded delegates there were. Apparently, coin tosses only needed to be recorded if the caucus site chose to use this new-fangled thing called an app to report results, and many delegates were reported by phone. Hmm… it was almost as if people didn't trust the app.

Anyway, after that bit of drama, Clinton won a squeaker, beating Sanders 49.8% to 49.6%. It was the beginning of a long campaign.

Chapter 26

Caucus Night 2020

Life in the weeks leading up to the Iowa caucus was still regular life. It was just life with wall-to-wall political ads on television, online, and even in the Yahtzee-knockoff app on my phone (where Tom Steyer had blanket coverage in hopes of winning the electronic dice game demographic). We also received enough junk mail to wallpaper a room as well as regular visits from campaign volunteers, so we weren't lonely. This all seemed like overkill to me, but I knew there were plenty of people who didn't pay much attention to the campaigns until the eve of the caucus, and there were no small number of undecideds, particularly with a field this large. It made sense for campaigns to come on strong in the end.

In the lead up to the caucus, the field also had shifted, as a "who's who" list of candidates I had seen had left the race. Just among candidates whose events I attended, those that dropped out were Cory Booker, Steve Bullock, Julián Castro, John Delaney, Bill di Blasio, Kirstin Gillibrand, Kamala

Harris, John Hickenlooper, Beto O'Rourke, Joe Sestak, Eric Swalwell and Marianne Williamson. There was an even longer "who's that?" list of minor or fringe candidates, which made me thankful that I never promised to see every single candidate for this project. But even with all these changes, there were more than a dozen people still in the race.

However, because life was still regular life, the night of the caucus was a busy one for us. I was cooking dinner while Devin was having her piano lesson and Ian was taking a shower after track practice. Julie had to leave early because she was volunteering to help the Elizabeth Warren campaign at the caucus site, so she was eating in the kitchen, and we discovered that one of the cats had thrown up on the stairs while Nic had just gotten back into town for the caucus and wanted to go early with Julie. So, yeah, a lot was happening.

But eventually, I was ready to leave with Devin by my side, and she was excited to be attending her first caucus. We bundled up and headed outside into the early February winter. As we made our way onto the street, I realized that my neighbors' garbage cans were lining the street, and I would have to remember to put mine out as well. Devin noted that the route we were taking to the caucus was the same that she had walked for the first six years of her life as a student, since our caucus site was still her old elementary school. It was a place we knew well, having had at least one child enrolled there for 15 years straight.

When we arrived, we could already see that parking was tight. At the school, there was as much happening in the lobby as on a student-teacher conference night. After spending several caucuses in the cafeteria, I was pleased to see that this year our precinct was going to be in the gymnasium, which was larger, and a different precinct had that honor of being housed in the cafeteria. I recognized the person behind us in the line. Like a character from an early chapter of a novel who returns for the climax, it was Dave, the owner of Octopus, the local bar where

I had earlier gone to see Montana Governor Steve Bullock. I found out that Dave was still undecided. I noted to him that he was running out of time to make up his mind. He agreed, and then we realized he was in the wrong line, so he left for the cafeteria queue.

Another returning figure from an earlier chapter was the t-shirt I had bought when I saw Colorado Senator Michael Bennett at a Raygun store in Cedar Rapids. I had finally found the perfect event to wear it to, though throughout the night a couple of people told me that Raygun had released another version of the shirt crossing out the names of candidates who had dropped out before the caucus. It was very difficult to keep on top of Iowa fashion trends.

The line moved slowly but steadily until we got inside the gymnasium where I had been dozens and dozens of times for music performances, talent shows, and assemblies. In fact, I immediately noticed that the chairs were set up exactly as if this was to be a 3rd grade chorus concert. We snaked our way toward the check-in tables where we were given double-sided Preference cards, which were designed to make things easier this year. I took mine, but I remained skeptical.

And then we were in, but I knew better than to get too excited. Nothing would be happening for a while. Devin saw a friend from school, and immediately ditched me. Around the gymnasium, I was surrounded by people from the neighborhood: friends, colleagues, former students and plenty of people I somehow had never seen before in my life even though we all live within walking distance of each other.

I should point out that another one of the many ways in which caucusing is nothing like voting is that most people were wearing stickers indicating which candidate they supported. I couldn't help but walk around the room sizing up my neighbor's decisions—*She supports Klobuchar; that makes sense. I can't believe he's with Warren; I thought he was a Republican.*— I'm sure people were having the same thoughts about me.

This is probably the point at which I should spill the beans as to how our family's support broke down. There were some twists and turns throughout the process. Nic had been an intern for Harris's campaign before she dropped out. Julie was a strong Booker supporter, and she was sorry to see him leave the race. They both wound up in the Warren camp, as did Devin who had been leaning her way since the very first political event we attended this season. Conversely (ironically?), I had been in the Warren camp for much of the fall and winter, and then, for reasons not even clear to me, I realized I would be supporting Sanders again, as I did during the 2016 caucus. There was no epiphany moment for me, and Warren remained my number two, but I felt I had made the right decision, even though it meant I had to gaze across the full length of the gymnasium to see the rest of my caucusing family members. We were a house divided yet again.

To capture the effect of my forlorn gaze across the room, I should explain how the gym was set up. While the center of the floor had chairs lined up and facing the stage, along the walls each campaign was given a small piece of real estate next to random gym class equipment that had been pushed up along the wall, though this is best represented through a little photo tour I put together, following a clockwise arc from the right side of the stage.

Under the east basketball hoop, with good signage: Pete Buttigieg.

Bernie Sanders gets the slot in front of the mileage club wall.

This Amy Klobuchar supporter was a first-time caucus goer.

Andrew Yang supporters will be in front of the mini-trampolines.

Sometimes a billion dollars only gets you a spot behind the parallel bars: Tom Steyer.

I had missed the Deval Patrick spot at first, but it's there.

No one was sure what was in the blue storage bins by Joe Biden.

Proving that money can't buy everything, Mike Bloomburg has a sad, little corner behind a door.

It was just the luck of the draw, but Tulsi Gabbard has the coolest background.

Michael Bennet. I have no joke.

Elizabeth Warren supporters turned the exit into a stage. Effective but clearly a fire hazard.

Winner of the 1976 caucus: Uncommitted.

By this point, half an hour after the announced start time, I had run out of things and people to photograph, and I realized that all the many hours I had spent waiting for tardy candidates to show up for their events was merely training for this moment. I was in caucus-shape. When everyone finally was checked in, the doors were closed and the caucus was ready to begin, as the temporary chair called the event to order. He immediately and without opposition was elected permanent chair because, really, who else would want such a lousy gig for the night? Rules were announced, a letter from the state party was read, and a call went out for representatives of each campaign to give a short speech on behalf of candidates. Though I suspected this was more a measure of organization than viability, six campaigns were represented: Biden, Buttigieg, Klobuchar, Sanders, Warren and Yang. I was grateful that the speeches were sincere and short.

I thought we were ready to caucus, but no. Now, they had to count how many people were in the room. Why wasn't this done earlier, say, when people were checking in? Good question. I had estimated there were around 400 people in the room, though I'm not good at judging crowds. After taking longer than one would think was necessary, we were told that there were 361, which meant that the magic number for viability was 55.

How does all that work again? Time for a recap. To get delegates in this year's Iowa caucus, a campaign had to have the support of at least 15% (55 people) of the total number in the room (361). Through some formula that never fully made sense to me, our precinct had been assigned 15 delegates to the state convention at the start of the night, and we weren't going home until they were all assigned. If a campaign fell short of 55, it would be considered non-viable, and that candidate's supporters would have the option of supporting another candidate during realignment. Simple, see? Just stay with me. It will become more clear as we go along.

Once the magic number was announced, the dance began. Attendees were told to take their Preference cards and go to the section of the gym assigned to their chosen candidate. We stood up out of our chairs and shuffled along the floor, dividing by our allegiances. So, even though we had our Preference cards, we weren't supposed to fill them out yet (for reasons that will soon become clear). Organizers for each candidate began taking a count. This involved pushing everyone into a corner as close together as possible while someone stood up and tried to count the group. The Bernie supporters were a large enough contingent that that wasn't going to work, and we soon had to all raise our hands and each shout out the next number in the sequence when we were pointed at. It felt like the beginning of a gym class, which means that the setting was appropropriate at least.

Looking around the gym, it soon became clear that the viability threshold of 55 was going to be more than could be met by most campaigns, even those with organizers in the room. Only the Sanders and Warren groups, stationed kitty corner across the gym from one another, looked easily large enough, and the Biden section seemed surprisingly small. Both Yang and Klobuchar seemed short of the number needed as well. It was hard to tell if a mother with a young child standing in front of the Bennet sign was supporting him or just an adjacent Warren supporter trying to give her kid a little room to roam.

Suddenly, there was drama! The count for Buttigieg came up a handful of people short of viability. But because no one had filled out their Preference cards yet, a quick act of negotiation took place and some Klobuchar supporters agreed to cross over to Buttigieg. A cheer went up to greet the converts. Meanwhile, a woman standing next to me in the Sanders group tried to woo members of the Yang gang, who were positioned next to us in the gym. She first made note of the candidates' shared support for Medicare For All, and then playfully offered hugs. The

Yang organizer scowled at all of this. Even if a candidate was not going to be viable, the initial number of supporters would be recorded, and organizers for three non-viable candidates, Biden, Klobuchar and Yang, were like sheepdogs trying to protect their lambs.

I may not have all the details right in the next part of this because it got pretty confusing. At some point, people were told that now they could fill out the #1 side of their Preference cards. So far, so good. Sanders-supporting parents of young children began asking if they could leave now. Apparently not, because the initial hand count for viability had to match the number of cards. This was almost impossible to ensure, because we'd been in the gym for over an hour by this point and some people clearly began slipping away, or they just got tired of standing at some point and went back to the middle of the gym. At one point, a woman with a bright green Klobuchar shirt handed me a Preference card from a Biden supporter and asked me to walk it over. Why me? Why was the card not handed in earlier? I don't know. Still wearing my Bernie sticker, I walked the card over, doing my part for party unity.

Eventually, the cards got turned in for the official count, and I finally saw the logic of the Preference cards. In the past, even after the first alignment count, people could flip candidates. Now, if your candidate was viable, your written down first preference was official and could not be changed. It also meant that if you were paying for a babysitter and your candidate was viable, you could go home. Plenty of people did just that as those of us that remained milled around waiting for the count. People broke out of their preference groups and began chatting again. I found myself standing with a Political Science professor as we teamed up to try and explain the impending realignment process to a journalist from the Netherlands. We did what we could. Meanwhile, people were getting texts from their friends in the adjacent precinct a room away in the cafeteria. They had already finished up for the night and had awarded their delegates (Sanders 5, Warren 4, Buttigieg 3, Klobuchar 3). It felt like we were in the class that got into trouble and had to stay after school.

Finally, the official first round count was announced. This was the initial tally of supporters (we weren't even close to assigning delegates yet) from our precinct:

Sanders 141

Warren 75

Buttigieg 58

Biden 24

Yang 23

Klobuchar 22

Steyer 4

Uncommitted 3

Gabbard 2

Bennet 0

Bloomberg 0

Patrick 0

Only three candidates had reached the viability threshold (Sanders, Warren, Buttigieg), which meant that they would be the only candidates getting delegates from our precinct tonight. But, that didn't mean we were done. It just meant it was time for realignment, and the fun was just starting.

For the next 15 minutes, supporters of non-viable candidates could choose to support someone else. Meanwhile, other people began putting away chairs as if the 3rd grade chorus concert was over. As organizers zipped around the gym, I heard a rumor that now-released Biden, Yang and Klobuchar supporters were going to try to join forces and create an Uncommitted group that could be viable, and, if it worked, then they would apparently arm wrestle over who got which delegates later. This was a terrible idea but not an impossible one. If you added up all the round one supporters of those candidates, that came to 69, which would have been enough to reach viability. However, these weren't sports teams with uniforms and managers. They were caucus goers that would have to be persuaded rather than ordered.

Nevertheless, the Uncommitted group made a run at it, while a chant of "make your vote count!" went up to discourage them. In the end, only about 25 people initially joined this action, and when it became clear that it wasn't going to fly, people began drifting away. My sense was that the Yang and Klobuchar supporters realigned elsewhere, while the Biden supporters were going to take their ball and go home.

Toward the end of realignment, I went back over to the Sanders section and sat next to a friend who started with Klobuchar, came over to Bernie briefly when Klobuchar didn't appear viable but stuck with Amy through the first count. Then she joined the Uncommitted group as part of that attempt. When it failed, she came back over to Bernie, but mainly she just wanted to sit down by that point.

Now, people who had realigned themselves could sign the #2 side of their Preference card, and they could go home as well. I saw the wisdom of this model, as it locked in support without making people wait around through all the counting. However, it also meant that most people went home without knowing the results. All that remained were the organizers (one of whom I was worried about because she hadn't eaten dinner and was clearly low blood sugar) and "there until the bitter end" folks like me who were going to stick around for the results.

As the realignment card count took place, the tone of the event changed. The gym had largely emptied out. No one needed to stay with their candidate group any longer. The time for political allegiances has passed. Now we were just shooting the breeze. The reporter from the Netherlands has been told about every Dutch person living in Cedar

Falls. We shared stories of caucuses past. We caught up with neighbors and friends. We talked about our childhoods.

Somehow I failed to record the vote tallies from the second round. I guess maybe I was a little low blood sugar as well. But when the numbers were official, the calculators came out and people crowded around a table at the front of the stage to work out the delegate counts. There was some confusion as the coordinator said he couldn't get the app to work on his phone to report the delegates, but he had someone from the state party on speakerphone and they were trying to figure things out (clever readers among you will recognize the foreshadowing in that last sentence). There was notable tension in the air as it all came down to how the 15 delegates were to be awarded. Similar math exercises were taking place or had already happened in every precinct in the state.

When they had finally figured it out and all the organizers agreed with the chair that the rules were being followed correctly, the final results were announced: Sanders 7, Warren 4, Buttigieg 4. It was a good night for Sanders. He held the precinct he had won in 2016 as well. Biden's lack of viability was somewhat unexpected. But the real surprise was that after just barely hitting the initial threshold, Buttigieg had tied Warren with four delegates each. Through some combination of realignment from the Biden and Klobuchar camps and rounding up, Buttigieg did better in our precinct than I would have expected. However, was this a good thing? Had it been a straight up vote, like in a primary, Buttigieg would have been under 15%, but he was going to walk away with more than 25% of the delegates. In the caucus model, a block of moderates were able to coalesce around one candidate. It's hard for me to definitively say one result would have been more fair than the other.

But don't leave yet! It ain't over. The organizers went into sheepdog mode and rounded up all the stragglers so that we could officially vote for the delegates and alternates to the county convention where they would vote for delegates to the state convention where they would vote for delegates to the national convention. We cast our lots again, this time with a small group of hand raisers and unanimous votes. By this point, Julie and Devin had already gone home. Nic and I stuck it out, and I got to take a picture of us in the elementary school gym he had run around in as a little kid. But when they announced to the shrivelled crowd that they would now begin accepting resolutions for the party convention platform, even we had had it. We bundled back up, walked home, and you'll be glad to know that I remembered to put the garbage can out.

That's where things were supposed to end, but as you know, they didn't. Results were delayed and then delayed again. TV news anchors couldn't hide their frustration as they found themselves with little to talk about. Soon, it emerged that there was a problem with a new app that was supposed to be used to report votes (the one that hadn't been working at our precinct). That would have been bad enough, but the back-up phone reporting system was also overwhelmed (and intentionally sabotaged by pro-Trump internet trolls clogging up the phone lines).

We stayed up watching and waiting, but there were no results that night. There were no results the next day. And when there were final results, people questioned them and, the AP refused to recognize the party-certified results. I had left the caucus site wondering if my precinct's results would be in any way predictive. Would Sanders do well? Would Buttigieg coalesce a moderate bloc? Would Biden do as poorly statewide? Those questions faded as others reared up. Would a winner be named? Would the results be certified? Would this be the last caucus in Iowa?

Let the giant game of musical chairs begin!

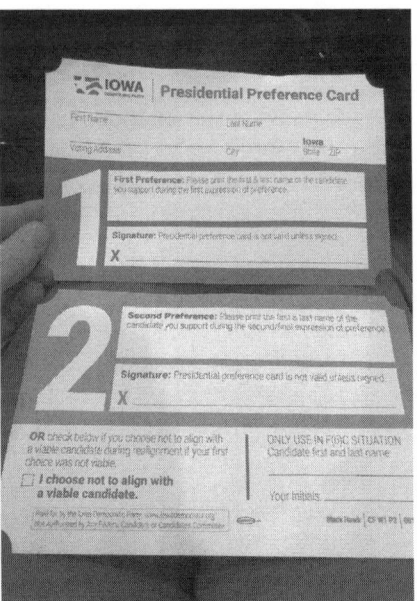
The Preference card

You'd never guess we'd been there 2 ½ hours.

There until the end.

Conclusion

The Last Caucus in Iowa

So, what the hell happened?

Well, the cliché had always been that there were "three tickets out of Iowa," which meant the point of the caucus was not to predict the future winner but to narrow the field to the most promising trio of candidates. But really, that was not what the rest of the country wanted. What the rest of the country wanted was something like the 2008 experience with Obama, where a candidate rose to the top, hit his or her stride, and went on to acquire an aura of inevitability.

That sure wasn't the case in 2020. Though, as I write, Joe Biden is the presumptive nominee, he did very poorly here, and the "three tickets out" cliché didn't play out either. Because of the uncertainty of the outcome, no one dropped out before the New Hampshire primary. Even though the results were claimed as a victory by Buttigieg (most delegates) and Sanders (most votes), things remained unsettled enough that all candidates were able to spin them. The perennial complaints about the Iowa Caucuses gained traction.

In the aftermath of caucus night, "Iowa" became a term of derision in the national media, and terms like "chaotic," "meltdown" and "disaster" were tossed around freely. I found myself wondering if that was what it was like to be a Floridian during the "hanging chad" and "butterfly ballot" controversies of the 2000 Presidential election. As I followed my Iowan friends on social media, I noticed that we all got our hackles up a bit. Here's why: one would have been hard pressed to find anyone here who didn't think the caucus process was kind of weird and that there were some inherent problems in the system. However, lost in all the hubbub was the fact that a couple of the changes in the system—the Preference cards and locking in first round support for viable candidates—were big improvements and ensured that there was a reliable record of the vote in a way that hadn't existed before. And it wasn't as if other states had found some magic formula for quickly calculating results. Both Nevada and California would go on to have delays in reporting results; however, neither of those states had contests that were too close to call initially. But because Iowa's results were close and a winner couldn't be declared on election night, its delays loomed larger in the public mind.

All that is true, but it is also not the whole story because of "the app." As you likely know, one of the innovations of the 2020 Iowa Caucus was to use a smartphone app created by a company almost-comically named Shadow, Inc. to report results, and the app was a flop. Precinct officials had trouble getting it to work (I saw this at my precinct), and when it did work it seemed to report out inaccurate results, and then the backup phone reporting system was overwhelmed. It took days before anything resembling a complete tally could be made. So, yeah, that was a mess, but a bad app was just a technical problem for which there could be a technical solution.

What was more significant, but received less coverage, was what happened when reporters began drilling down into the individual precinct results. In the past, all that precincts reported out were delegate numbers, which weren't that complicated (i.e. 7 Obama, 5 Clinton, 2 Edwards).

There was no record of the calculations done behind the scenes to get to that point. And as my informal account of my 2008 precinct showed, the numbers were not always exact. After the close caucus results in 2016, the Preference cards were introduced in an effort to be more transparent.

That worked. There now was a more meaningful way of checking the results. But what that revealed was how awry the process could go on a precinct-by-precinct level, not through any intentional efforts, but because the caucus process was so complicated. I can imagine many future graduate student dissertations emerging from the available data, as in just one *New York Times* article, "Iowa Caucus Results Riddled With Errors and Inconsistencies," the reporters were able to find—well, you saw the headline. Because there were hard numbers for initial preferences, final preferences and delegate awards, the numbers could be checked for accuracy. But this is the key takeaway from that article:

"Just about every election night includes reporting errors. They can be difficult to identify, but can often be corrected during a recount or a postelection canvass. This year's Iowa caucuses are the reverse: Errors are now easy to identify, and hard to correct."

Ay, there's the rub. In an election, if a mistake is found, it can be fixed. But in a caucus, though the errors could be identified this year, correcting them was almost impossible because of the multi-stage process built into the caucus. To wit (hey, maybe I should use Shakespearean quotes for this whole explanation!), viable candidates shouldn't have lost any voters after realignment, but the *Times* found that that happened in 10 precincts. After the initial alignment, no new voters should be allowed to join, but in at least 70 precincts, that happened. These errors can be identified but there is no way to address them after the fact. "Lord, what fools these mortals be!"

But was that it? No. "There are more things in heaven and earth, Horatio, than are dreamt of in your philosophy." There were precincts that awarded more delegates than they were supposed to. In at least 15 cases, one candidate receiving more votes than another candidate in the final alignment was awarded fewer delegates. And then there were honest tabulation errors like the one that made it appear that Deval Patrick had won a Des Moines precinct. It would have taken a robust reporting system to confirm all results before they were reported, in line with Romeo's advice: "Go wisely and go slowly. Those who rush stumble and fall."

So, what does the Iowa caucus look like from a distance? Well, though Shakespeare (last quote, I promise!) would say "what's gone and what's past help should be past grief," you may rightly come away from this thinking at least "well, that ain't right." I agree. The 2020 Iowa caucus was a flawed process, though not because of corruption or because Iowans weren't committed to trying to make it work. In the big picture of American democracy, it may be pretty far down the list of things that are flawed—coming in behind unregulated political contributions, the electoral college, voter suppression and gerrymandering—but that doesn't make it right. With voter suppression on the rise and efforts to undermine the very act of voting underway, the legitimacy of any electoral system matters, and there are reasons to worry about the legitimacy of the caucus system. If the caucus can't be done right, it shouldn't be done.

However, there are things to celebrate about Iowa's system. Having an early race in a small, inexpensive state means candidates have to actually work the field and can't just try to buy the nomination (though that doesn't stop some from trying). Many Iowans take the caucus and Iowa's first-in-the-nation status seriously and make considered decisions because of that. That matters more than ever in the post-Citizens United era, when billionaires can throw unfathomable amounts of money into races.

So, I don't have a crystal ball that would allow me to see what the future will bring, but at this moment there is one issue that, more than any others, might determine the fate of the caucus, and that is COVID-19.

At the time of the caucus (1 February 2020) Coronavirus concerns were just starting to make their way into the national discussion, though we now know intelligence sources were aware of its potential impact even then. We are in the midst of the pandemic as I'm writing, and it is not clear what the end result will be, other than that the loss of life has been horrific and the social and economic impact will be felt for years.

The concerns of the moment are much bigger than the fate of the Iowa caucus, and it is not impossible that the desire to "get back to normal" will be so strong that there will be an effort to preserve as much of our pre-COVID-19 world as possible. However, it is more likely that life after the pandemic will continue to be shaped by our experience of it (even when/if a vaccine becomes available).

As I reviewed my photos of this process, I couldn't help but have a visceral reaction to the crowded bars and halls, the many handshakes and hugs, and the packed gymnasium where I attended the 2020 caucus. How much of that will continue to be part of our culture? When will we feel comfortable being pressed against one another for a political event? And will such things become the exception rather than the rule?

Also, as I am writing this, there are concerns about the physical process of voting. Calls have been issued for greater use of mail-in voting, particularly in the aftermath of Wisconsin's refusal to cancel its in-person primary. Voters were forced to go to the polls in that state, and several dozen contracted COVID-19 simply by refusing to allow their votes to be suppressed. But while mail-in ballots offer a safe solution to the problem of voting, there is no way to have a socially-distanced caucus. Unless we will all feel comfortable standing toe to toe with one another, something will have to change.

There is good reason to wonder if this will, in fact, be the Last Caucus in Iowa. If so, I'm glad I had a chance to participate and have this unique experience. As quirky as it was, I took it seriously, as did many of my friends and neighbors. Of course, that's not to say a different state, a state with a more diverse population, couldn't do the same. Iowa Caucus, glad to have known you. If you come back in four years, I'll be there waiting for you.

Jim O'Loughlin is the author of the flash fiction collection *Dean Dean Dean Dean* (Twelve Winters Press) and editor of *Kurt Vonnegut Remembered* (University of Alabama Press). He founded and hosts the Final Thursday Reading Series, which is celebrating its 20th season.

The Ice Cube Press began publishing in 1991 along the Kaw River to focus on how to live with the natural world and to better understand how people can best live together in the communities they share and inhabit. Using the literary arts to explore life and experiences in the heartland of the United States we have been recognized by a number of well-known writers including: Bill Bradley, Gary Snyder, Gene Logsdon, Wes Jackson, Patricia Hampl, Greg Brown, Jim Harrison, Annie Dillard, Ken Burns, Roz Chast, Jane Hamilton, Daniel Menaker, Kathleen Norris, Janisse Ray, Craig Lesley, Alison Deming, Harriet Lerner, Richard Lynn Stegner, Richard Rhodes, Michael Pollan, David Abram, David Orr, Tom Brokaw, and Barry Lopez. We've published a number of well-known authors including: Mary Swander, Jim Heynen, Mary Pipher, Bill Holm, Connie Mutel, John T. Price, Carol Bly, Marvin Bell, Debra Marquart, Ted Kooser, Stephanie Mills, Bill McKibben, Craig Lesley, Elizabeth McCracken, Derrick Jensen, Dean Bakopoulos, Rick Bass, Linda Hogan, Pam Houston, and Paul Gruchow. Check out Ice Cube Press books on our web site, join our email list, Facebook group, or follow us on Twitter. Visit booksellers, museum shops, or any place you can find good books and support true honest to goodness independent publishing projects so you can discover why we continue striving to "hear the other side."

Ice Cube Press, LLC (Est. 1991)
North Liberty, Iowa, Midwest, USA
Resting above the Silurian and Jordan aquifiers
steve@icecubepress.com
check us out on twitter and facebook
www.icecubepress.com

To Fenna Marie, the all-time "GK"!
truly a voter since the beginning!